I0186921

Time Will Tell

Dalarse Shannon Demby

Copyright © 2016 Dalarse Shannon Demby

All rights reserved.

ISBN: 1732092605
ISBN-13: 978-1-7320926-0-0

DEDICATION

This Book Is dedicated to anybody carrying the weight of the world on their shoulders. Set it down.

ACKNOWLEDGEMENTS

First and Foremost, I'd like to thank god for blessing me with the talent to write. I'd also like to thank my mother Earlene Anne Edwards A.K.A. "Bubbie" for all of the countless letters we wrote back and forth because sometimes conversations were uncomfortable. Thanks for giving me an outlet. I'd like to thank my sons for serving as motivation. Sadiek I finished this book just to make you proud. Ahmad and Curran I love you. To my brothers Bryant thank you for your brutal honesty! Sas, thanks for constantly bugging me to get it done, Booge thanks for being my Coach, all of those "Let's go's" & "Get to works" got me through this. To my sisters Naya thanks for your excitement and feedback. that gave me that courage to put my work out here and Porsche thanks for your continued love and support. Destiny, I'm glad you're back. To my cousins you know who you are. Thanks for being so amazing that I decided to be too! Dad, I have always felt that I got my creativity from you. Me in the lab is equivalent to you in the kitchen. Thanks

Last but not least, to my Husband Carnell, thank you a million times for the million nights that you listened to me read aloud, the million scenes you acted out, the million time you gave your input and for putting up with my attitude

CHAPTER ONE

James Crenshaw was born and raised on the streets of Philadelphia. He was six feet, 5 inches tall with caramel skin, brown eyes and had always been teased that he should have played basketball. James' had only made it to the 10th grade, not because he was dumb but because he felt that college was a waste of time for a black man such as himself. He was a product of his, so he felt to survive he had to go hard and which he did. James became a parent automatically at the age of nineteen, to his little sister Jasmine. His mother who used to be stable suddenly became a drug addict which James didn't quite understand. Yes he did sell drugs on the street but he never used it as he needed his head leveled. Sometimes he felt the death of his mom's best friend, Sasha's mom contributed to their mother's substance abuse. Even though his mother was a dope fiend and didn't know or didn't tell them who their father was, he still loved her.

There were two main crews in the dope game, or at least only two that mattered. The crews were run by James Crenshaw and his rival Jamal

Johnson. James unlike Jamal, was doing what he felt was necessary to get his family out of the hood. And that's exactly what he planned to do. Whose world is this he rapped along with Nas while parking to meet up with Ant. He would provide for his family by any means, he thought as he walked down to their stash spot looking for Ant.

"Yo! Ant, wad up?" James yelled as he walked up to Ant from behind.

"My Nigga! Wad up J?" Ant replied.

"Chilling as always, you saw Tone?" James asked.

"Yeah, about thirty minutes ago. He was just out here asking if you were around." Ant replied.

Ant was also raised on the streets of Philadelphia just like James. He was James childhood friend and right hand man. James took care of him like he was his brother, and because of that there wasn't anything that Ant wouldn't do for James. He grew in Blumberg projects with his mom and sister. His mother was a trick, not a self-proclaimed trick, but the hood knew her. She had never worked a day in her life, not to mention she's still stuck in the 90's. As a kid, she would go missing for days while Ant and his sister stayed home alone starving. Even as a kid James always made sure they were fed. James was 2 years older than Ant but they were pretty close in size, so he always had fresh clothes to wear and Sasha always looked out for his little sister Deja. Deja was gorgeous, and so ambitious, but ended up getting mixed up with the wrong crowd. She started running with a group of hot ass girls from 25th and Norris. They were Notorious for setting up local Kingpins. She got involved with the wrong person and it costed her life... Her body was found two days before her 21st birthday in Fairmount Park. Ant was devastated and had never felt so alone. Don't get it twisted; Ant was a beast, and a math magician. Back in the day he'd adopted the nickname Math, and that's the role he played on James team. He knew where, how and why to move dope, and in order to maximize on his talent. The ShawStoppers as they called themselves, needed access to the entire city, and there was no better place to start than with Jamal's crew and corners.

"Oh ard, hopefully for his sake he had my money. I called his nut ass twice today." James said a little frustrated. He had been trying to reach Tone for a while now, but to no avail.

"There he go right there coming out of the store." Ant said, calling James' attention.

"Tone!" James yelled. "That's him? That nigga look bad, what's up with him?" James asked Ant.

"Shit! You know exactly what's wrong with him, he been testing the product." Ant replied.

"Ay yo Tone!" James yelled again and this time Tone heard and started to run the moment he recognized it was James. "TONE! Shit! Motherfucker!" James screamed and started to run after him.

Tone used to run with James crew doing little shit like drop offs and running errands. He got dropped for fucking up the money on a consistent basis.

"Where the fuck did that nigga go." Ant said out of breath from running.

"Damn Ant, I didn't know you were that fast." James said as he sat on a vacant step to catch his breath. "Ima catch that nigga!" James said out of frustration.

"You good dawg?" Ant asked, "I thought you were something like an all-American." He teased and laughed. "You winded as shit my nigga" Ant said.

"That was a long time ago nigga. Only thing I'm running these days is numbers fam!" James replied laughing.

"I feel you on that" Ant replied.

"I ain't got time to be hitting the gym like that no more. I gotta make sure Jas is straight, you feel me?" James said still panting.

Ant looked away for a while as he had something on his mind to tell James.

"Yeah nigga I been meaning to talk to you about Jas." Ant said with a little heaviness as he knew that he had to tread lightly when speaking of Jas.

"What the fuck about her?" James snapped.

Ant shook his head as if to say, 'I knew it'. "Damn nigga, would you calm down? Shit!" Ant said.

"Well talk!" James snapped again wondering Ant could be all about.

"Look, I just been hearing her name a lot down 21st St, where them young bulls be hanging at."

"Oh yeah, and which one of them niggas said her name." James asked angrily. "What the fuck could them ass grown niggas, have to say about her?" James said as he paced with his fist clenched.

"Well, nine times out of ten it's because she's hanging with grown ass Taylor." Ant said with his face turned up, knowing he was going to defend Taylor too, regardless of the truth.

"Chill dawg, that's family too, plus I thought Sasha was keeping a pretty cool handle on her." James said.

"Man, she acts like an angel around y'all, but she's far from an angel bro." Ant said.

"What you trying to say?" James asked, slightly irritated.

Ant's uneasiness was very obvious on his face. "Man there ain't no easy way to say this, but on the low she hitting every nigga with a nice car. Real shit bro." Ant said calmly.

"Aye yo! Don't say no shit like that to me, man!" James said.

"It's the truth J, you know I got mad respect for you and Sash, too much to ever speak about her like that, unless it was true!" Ant said, taking a step back.

"Damn, I gotta talk to Sasha; make sure she know what's going on. She got too much on her plate as it is." James said, with a worried look. Ant smiled and teased.

"Whatever Nigga, you just want a reason to talk to her."

"Shut up dawg! Let's go handle this business so I can go holla at Sasha." James said with a mild smile, knowing there was a little truth in what he said. Sasha was not just his best friend but a woman he loved.

"Yo, can I ask you one question?" Ant said

"Yeah, what's up? Answered James

"You ain't hit that yet" Ant asked smiling

"Fuck you!" James said smiling and turning his face away.

"I'm just asking, she is bad a shit and y'all always together. So I know you hit that already. Didn't you J?" Ant said.

"Mind your business nigga, and stay the fuck away from her." James said slightly serious, even though he knew Sasha would never give him the time of day.

"Oh I know better nigga, I see how you be looking at her all dazed and in love and shit." Ant continued teasing with the truth.

"Dawg you tripping." James said laughing.

"Yeah ok, I hear you. Anyway, where we going first? I caught up with a few of them niggas earlier. So we only gotta see Rock and Mike cause you know Broady gon meet me at the spot." Ant said.

"Ard Bet" James said.

"Where your car at nigga? Ant asked.

"I'm right here on the corner. You kill me actin like you're too good to walk. Nigga it's two blocks away." James said, nudging him on the side.

"Yeah you right but that's a long way to run if somebody start dumping on us!" Ant said wide eyed. He had been on the street long enough to know that anything can go down at any time.

"True! True! Well let's just hurry up, I'm meeting up with Justine later." James said as they headed towards his car.

"Oh shit that fine ass girl we met at the bar the other night?" Ant asked.

"Yeah she been on my top HEAVY nigga! So I'mma go ahead and take her down tonight. You feel me?" James asked with a little pride. He had always been a ladies man, and he took great pride in it. They got into the car and drove off to see Rock.

"What's up fellas?" Rock said as James and Ant got out of the car.

"Aint shit" James said shaking his hand. Wassup with you?

"Not a mother fucking thing it's kinda slow around here today." Rock replied.

"Them motherfuckers probably still ain't come down from yesterday, we made a killing out here!" Ant said enthusiastically.

"Oh yeah?! That's what I like to hear." Rock said.

"Aye listen, I'm working on some big shit, Imma schedule a sit down in a few weeks to talk about expanding." James said.

"Schedule?" Ant said laughing. "What the fuck? You sounding like a fucking businessman." he teased. "We are businessmen, nigga you keep thinking like a runner and that's the problem.

I don't know about yall but I feel like it's time we become top dogs around here." James said.

"Hell Yeah" Rock replied.

"With that being said keep your eyes and ears open it's time to recruit a few more runners, to join Ant's nut ass!" They jokes.

Still laughing rock replied, "Mike came pass earlier and left his shit with me. Said he'll be out of town until tomorrow night or some shit." "Probably with freak ass Tamika." James said. "What Tamika?" Rock asked. "Tamika from 22nd street" James replied.

"Oh yeah, he getting down with her like that?" Rock asked.

"Yeah that nigga been fucking with her heavy." Ant replied.

"That nigga crazy." Rock said, as he they were about to enter the house.

James phone rang and he stopped at the door. "Go ahead I'll be in." James said as Sasha's number flashed across his screen. Ant shook his head as Rock wondered who it could be.

"Must be Sasha, that nigga get real serious when she call him." Ant said as they entered the house. "What's up Sash?" James said into the phone.

"Nothing was sup with you?" Sasha said into the phone.

"Nothing, I'm a little busy. You good?" he asked.

"Busy?" Sasha said into the phone, irritated.

"Yeah wassup." James said as he could read her mood through the phone.

"Where you at?" She asked

"I'm nearby Sash was sup?" James asked, now irritated too. Sasha always acted like his mother and wife at the same time, sometimes it felt good and other times it got on his fucking nerves. This was one of those times.

"Probably doing some stupid shit. I just wanted to

vent about Taylor, but its cool forget it."

"Sasha will you chill out, for once Damn! I will be there in like ten minutes, I ..." The phone went dead before he could even finish. "This fucking girl!" he yelled in frustration, got back in his car and drove off.

CHAPTER TWO

Sasha paced around the living room as she thought about what she was going to do about her younger sister, Taylor. Sasha is a twenty-one year old. She was a full time college student raising her fourteen year old sister just like James. Their mother Pam, died when she was fifteen by a hit and run driver. They never found out who killed her. All they knew was they were expecting a storm, and she'd left to go grocery shopping and never came home. The police investigated her mother's murder for like two months before they closed the case. It was then Sasha decided to school for her criminal justice degree. Jeanine, James mother took responsibility for them but it was all left to Sasha and James the moment she started slipping. Outside of school and working full time, she spends all of her extra time chasing her little sister around corners and trying to keep her away from the dirty neighborhood boys. James is probably the only person in this world that she's afraid of as she looks up to him like a big brother.

"Shit!" she said as her thoughts wandered to James. She had been in love with James since they were kids, but for fear of it ruining what they'd worked so hard to become they kept it clean.

Sash was five feet, ten inches and light brown

skin and deep blue eyes. She was slim but curvy with a shoulder length hair. Sasha had an effect on almost every guy she came in contact with, she was beautiful and the spitting image of her mother. Sometimes she wondered how James was able to resist all of her for so long. "Buzz!" the buzzer went off, bringing her back to reality.

"Sasha come open the door!" James said into the phone standing on her steps a little nervous. "As much as he has known Sasha all his life, he is still always nervous. Especially when she's is in bad mood. It wasn't that he was afraid of her. She was just too much for him, and he realized that. She was the total package. She possessed all the quality you'd look for in a wife. She was smart and sexy, and slightly ratchet. She had goals and morals. This made him respect her more. He knew she loved him too and he hated that he couldn't give her what she wanted, but he also knew that he wasn't ready.

She opened the door with her hands folded across her chest with a little attitude.

"What's up with you, why are you tripping on me? He

asked with a smile.

"I'm not. I called to talk to you because I'm tired of chasing Taylor's grown ass around the city." She said as she turned around walking away from the door. James' eyes went straight to her ass unconsciously, before coming back up to meet her eyes. She smirked and lifted her eyebrow.

"What's crazy is I was coming to talk to you about some shit I heard about her today too." James said. "Yeah I've been hearing shit too." Sasha said and sighed.

"For how long?" James asked.

"For a few months now I just didn't want to bother you." She said dropping into the chair.

"You know you should have called me." James said as he sat next to her. When it came to Jasmine and Taylor even though they were their sisters, they were more like their children. They called on each other when they couldn't handle their sisters. When Jasmine got her period he sent her over to Sasha and when Taylor first got caught cutting school and hanging with guys Sasha sent her to James. Taylor knew not to play with James when it came to school and that was why it surprised me that she was cutting up school. "So wassup with her? What has she been doing now?" James asked, tired.

"For starters, she hasn't been going to school. Then she's been dealing with some nigga named Brian from around 16th street" Sasha explained.

"What Brian with the green LeSabre? James asked. "Yeah that him, he got a brother named Tone right?" Sasha asked.

"Yup that's him; he's 20 fucking years old. Sasha replied

What the hell does he want with a 14 year old girl?" James asked with frustration. He got up from his chair and began to pace. All he could think of was that Tone and his whole family was disrespecting him. "I'm definitely gonna deal with Brian and his crack head ass brother." He thought to himself.

"Where is she at now?" James asked. "I don't know. First her teacher called here earlier to tell me that Taylor hasn't been to her English class in two weeks. So I take off work to go up there and they tell me she hasn't even swiped her damn ID card in two weeks. I leave there and go looking for her at your house and her girlfriend Shante's house and she's nowhere to be found. By the time I make it back home and there is some girl on my line named Sheena telling me that when she catches Taylor, she is going to put her foot in her ass. All of this bullshit because of some lame ass nigga she calls her man." Sasha continued to rant, exhausted.

"This little girl is nothing but drama." James said.

"Of course I told the bitch, she better not touch my sister. But I can't really be mad at her because she and the lame nigga got a little boy together." Sasha replied.

"Well who is this nigga?" he asked. "I don't know but I just feel like she could have called me as a woman. These girls be bugging over these niggas."

James could not believe all he was hearing about Taylor. So Ant was telling the truth, he thought to himself. "You should have fucking called me and told me that she was cutting up like this." James said dropping his head into his hands.

"Yeah I know. I thought I had everything under control." Sasha shrugged.

James stood up, brought out his phone and began scrolling through it. "What you doing?" Sasha asked. "I'm about to send PJ over to that nigga crib to take care of him and to bring Taylor's ass home. Because I bet you that's where her ass is, well shit hopefully"

"So you're leaving?" Sasha asked

"Nah I'm staying right here. Aye did you check on Jas while you were up at the school?" James asked as an afterthought.

"Would I check on one without the other?" She responded sarcastically with her left brows up.

"Ok, and?" he asked. "Well Jas has missed a few days as well but not nearly as many days as Taylor and all of her work is caught up. She is probably following Taylor. You know Jas isn't like that." Sasha said trying to defend Jasmine. James got more pissed because he expected Jasmine to be more responsible.

"No she is like that if she missed days. If she wasn't like that she'd be telling Taylor to get her shit together or coming to one of us." James flipped.

"Come on now be real James they ain't telling on each other."

"Yeah well let me call PJ." James said as he put the phone to his ear. PJ was a part of James' crew member and he trusted him to handle Taylor with care. He filled PJ in and asked him to head over to Brian's house and check if both girls were there.

"What the fuck? What type of motherfucker would do that?" PJ vented over the phone.

"I know right." James said.

PJ said he'd head straight over and hit James back once he had something.

Within 15 minutes he called back and James told him to stay on the phone because he wanted to hear what Brian had to say.

"Yo motherfucker! You niggas have a habit of talking shit when I ain't around and messing with my sisters?" James yelled into the phone. He could hear Brian apologize and make up excuses. He knew PJ was beating him up real good especially with the way Brian screaming and hollering.

"Stop, you're hurting him!" Taylor screamed in the background. "Yo J! On my way to you" PJ said. "Good looking fam, so me a favor and pick up Jas because I'm sure that Taylor knows exactly where she is. When one suffers they both suffers." PJ arrived in 30 minutes and as soon as he smelled the food, he immediately tried to go in. Sasha had already made his plate so James passed it to him through the door.

"Good looking dawg. I'll get with you tomorrow." James said staring Jas and Taylor down. James and PJ shook hands and off he went, while both girls just stood there outside. "Come in don't just stand there looking stupid, the jig is up." James said. Before they could even make to the James started firing questions at them. While Sasha just stared at them especially Taylor furiously.

"Taylor who is Brian?" James asked.

"I don't know." Taylor replied with an attitude. Before James could ask another question Sasha slapped Taylor across the face. Jas moved just out of the way just in case she was next.

"Taylor how was school?" James asked.

"It was fine." Taylor said, still hold her face. She flinched expecting another one, knowing she'd lied. "Taylor, I was on the phone with PJ when he came to get y'all. So stop all of this lying." James said.

"He's just some boy that I like." She stuttered.

"He's not a boy, he's a twenty year old man and what the fuck were you doing in his house?" James said. "You are fourteen fucking years old." Sasha yelled from behind.

"It wasn't like that, that was my first time over there and I just wanted something to drink." Taylor lied.

"Taylor don't fucking play with me, you live four blocks away you could have come home and got something the fuck to drink." James barked, Taylor was really getting on his nerves with all her lying. He turned to Jasmine,

"And you, Jasmine!" Jasmine almost jumped out of her seat when she heard her name. "Why the fuck have you been missing so many days at school?" he asked her furiously.

"I been" Jasmine mumbled.

"Jas if you lie Imma knock the shit out of you, understand?" James said even though he knew he wouldn't lay a finger on her.

"Yes." Jasmine replied almost trembling.

"Now where have you been?" "I have been going to Brian's house with Taylor somedays." Jasmine said, avoiding eye contact with Taylor.

"Some days what about the other days?" Sasha asked looking at Taylor with disappointment. "At Jason's." Jasmine replied.

"Who the fuck is Jason and how old is he?" James asked.

"James he's just a friend I swear and he's fifteen." Jasmine said.

"Then what the fuck are y'all doing during school hours that you can't do after school?"

"Nothing J, he doesn't go to school." Jasmine stuttered.

"He doesn't go to school? What the fuck you doing with a stupid nigga?" James asked.

"He ain't stupid, his mom is sick." James thought of slapping her but he could never leave with myself if he put his hands on her. He stared at them speechless,

"Y'all go upstairs. I want y'all in the house everyday straight from school. If I can't trust y'all to carry y'all selves, like young women, while giving y'all a little freedom, than there is no freedom. And Taylor please don't try me." James said.

James and Sasha just watched them go upstairs, he could hear them arguing on the way up the steps, James just chuckled and shook his head. In as much as he hated to admit it, they were no longer kids.

"You got some weed?" Sasha asked exhausted from grilling the girls.

"Yeah I got some, chill out." James said smiling.

"I can't chill out, J they drive me crazy. I swear to god, they better not leave this house for two weeks. I'mma give their asses fifteen minutes to get home from school every day." Sasha rambled on as he handed her the L. James enjoyed nights like this, when the stress wasn't about them. Years ago, they made a vow to each other that they would always look out for each other, and that no matter what, they would help the other out with their sibling so that they wouldn't ever want for anything. To uphold that promise Sasha was working two jobs and James hustling.

"Ay yo! You gotta stop slapping people like that. You used to do that shit to me when we was kids." James said as he nudged her in the side.

"Yeah because you are always trying to cop a free feel." Sasha said smiling.

"Whatever don't nobody want to feel on you?" James said.

"Yeah ok. So what's been going on with you? It seems like only the family drama brings you around these parts lately." Sasha noted.

"I was just thinking the same thing. I'm sorry it's just that I have been on my grind. Sash I'm so tired of this shit. I want out but I can't get out until I know that we are all right." James said.

"James I have told you that we are cool. If you get a legit job we would do better, you don't have to be out there in them streets like that." Sasha said.

Sasha had never really liked James being involved with selling drugs, even though it has always helped with expenses. It just didn't sit well with her.

"That legit shit ain't gonna work out for us right now. I'm paying rent at two places right now, I know you see them two high maintenance ass girls up there in that room." James said.

"So you gone to continue to grind and hope that you are not locked the fucked up or killed. Cause if that happens how many fucking legit jobs am I gonna need." Sasha said.

James rolled his eyes and said, "Here we go again. Sasha this is just why I been staying the fuck away from here because it's always this same shit."

"Oh so at first you was grinding now it's me, fuck you James! I'm going to bed." Sasha said. "

Sasha, why are you tripping? We sound like we married and we ain't even a couple. You knew what my goal was when I got in this shit! I gotta get us outta here. You, me, Jeanine all of us. Listen I want out but I gotta figure out a way." James said genuinely. She stood there with her arms folded across her chest, rolling her eyes at him.

James thought of changing the topic before it got out of hand fast. "What's up with that nut ass nigga Sam you been seeing?" James asked.

"I haven't been seeing anybody." Sasha said with an attitude.

"So you just gonna lie in my face knowing that my man saw you and that nigga at Fridays, last night. What you thought? He didn't tell me or did you think I wouldn't say anything?" James asked partly teasing and partly jealous.

"It wasn't even like that though J. I just needed company so I called him and we went out. We are not dating he's my classmate." Sasha said.

"Damn it's like that you just call niggas when you bored and they come to the rescue." James said rolling his eyes.

"First of all it ain't niggas it's just Saul, and his name

is Saul! And like I said it was nothing." Sasha said.

"Just Sam huh?" James said smirking, intentionally saying his name wrong in order to annoy her. "Oh so you and pretty boy serious? It all about him now huh?" James asked.

"You know what James this conversation is over, because you just gonna twist everything that I say to make it seem like something else." she said while rolling her eyes. James laughed as he dropped on a seat next to her.

"You trippin yo." James said as he laughed.

"Yeah you tripping." she replied. "So what we gonna do about the little hoochies upstairs?" James asked. "Keep whooping their asses until they get it right." Sasha said.

CHAPTER THREE

"I am like so fuckin sick of them actin like they're so perfect. Like they ain't never missed a class. Shit James is dropped out." Jasmine said as she sat on Taylor's bed.

"Right and Sasha thinks that just because she in college that everyone has to go. I'm telling you if she slaps me again Imma slap her ass back." Taylor said.

Jasmine burst into laughter as this was not the first time she would say such. "Shut up Taylor. You say that shit every time you get slapped. You ain't gonna do shit. You better learn how to duck." Jasmine said still laughing.

"Fuck you bitch Taylor replied quickly." Taylor was a pretty outspoken fourteen year old girl. She started having sex at the age of 12 and had several boyfriends. She loves her sister Sasha a lot but sometimes she felt her sister was too boring and was trying to make her the same way. She loved being a free bird especially since their mother died. She was five feet eight inches tall with a short haircut that in her opinion made her look like Halle Berry.

"I ain't trying to hear shit they talking about I

just can't wait to get back over there with Brian. Girl that nigga had me all twisted up before PJ brought his fine ass over there." Taylor said in a dreamy tone.

"Brian is the reason you just got the shit slapped, what's wrong with you? Jas asked. "And I'll get slapped a hundred times more, because that work he put in is everything!" Taylor said with a slutty look.

"You need to slow down Taylor. I have only been going over there with you hoping that y'all wouldn't do anything, because I was there."

"Now Bitch you tried it! You know I'm gon fuck regardless."

"Well I hope you being careful I know you ain't tryna get pregnant at 14." Jasmine said, truly worried about her wild friend.

"If it happens it's meant to happen." Taylor said as she took her clothes off.

"Oh bitch now you talking stupid. If you do get pregnant you betta be prepared to move out of this country cause James gon kill your ass." Jasmine said rolling her eyes.

Jasmine and Taylor are best friend but

they are totally different. Jasmine respects James and what he's doing for her and her family, Like James she wants to get out of the hood as well. She has hopes of going to college like Sasha, to study fashion design. She loved the art of looking good and has always dreamed of helping others look the same. Jasmine shied away from boys for the most part. But she was gorgeous and never had a problem getting their attention. She was about five feet, eight inches tall with long black hair that she mostly wore in a ponytail. She had dark beautiful eyes and full lips that made her smile contagious.

"Yeah, yeah, whatever. Come on let's go apologize so we can get out of here. Tierra having a party tonight and I know Brian gonna be there." Taylor said.

"Yeah and so is his baby momma Tia, like girl what are you just looking for trouble?" Jasmine asked.

"I don't give a fuck about that whore that ain't even his baby and if she start pushing up on my man imma knock that bitch out." Taylor said confidently like she could handle her all on her own.

"First off that isn't you're fucking man they have been together for like 6 years." Jasmine said, snapping her fingers to bring her to reality.

"Well he's mine now!" Taylor said.

"You are fucking sick."

"Ard chill come on let's go apologize." Taylor said.

"Oh y'all were kissing!" Jasmine said catching James and Sasha off guard.

"I thought I sent y'all dizzy asses upstairs." Sasha said, climbing out of James lap. "I hope y'all wasn't coming down here to try that apologizing shit cause it ain't gonna work this time. I heard about Tierra's party y'all ain't getting out of this house tonight. Now take y'all asses back upstairs." Sasha said reading their mind. Taylor and Jasmine angrily stomped back up the stairs. As they left James and Sasha smiled awkwardly at each other.

James had always tried to control his feelings so he was not even sure how the kiss happened. "How the hell did I kiss Sasha?" he thought to himself. They had kept their feelings under control for the last 7 years and hadn't kissed since they were kids. They were just sitting there talking about how far they had come and how they had to keep going and the kiss just happened. He looked at her again and he could feel himself leaning towards her again but he quickly stopped himself. "Sash I'm just gonna go chill wit Ant. Make sure that they stay they asses in this house and if they get out of hand, call me." James said getting to his feet.

"J I can handle them it's you that I can't handle." Sasha said.

"What are you talking about?" James asked confused

"You just said that you were gonna stay in with us tonight. Now you leaving. What the fuck is that about? Cause they caught us kissing? That shit wasn't no accident; we did exactly what we wanted to do." Sasha said a little bit pissed.

"Sash it ain't about that I just changed my mind."

"You are such a liar! One minute you the toughest nigga around and the next you running scared like a little bitch."

"You better watch your fuckin mouth." James said.

"Or what you gon hit me?" Sasha said standing to face

him.

"You know what, you're right! I don't even know why I'm letting you piss me off Sasha. Ima get out of here because it's the best thing for me to do right now." James said turning towards the door.

"Why is running away from the obvious. The best. What are you so afraid of J? You know how I feel about you and I know how you feel about me. This shit aint going away. We've been playing this game for damn near ten years now! & I'm tired of it!" Sasha said angrily.

"Me too Sash! I'm tired of it! We are supposed to be family! So what do you want from me? You want me to fuck you is that it? Treat you like some basic ass broad? I'm not ready to settled down, I'm not gonna be tied down to one girl! I'm not getting out of the game! Sash! I'm not getting a job! I'm not doing any of the shit that you want me to do, not right now! Why can't you get that? I can't be what you need." James said out of frustration.

Sasha's face went blank and sad. She blinked fast and dropped her head. James felt bad and couldn't believe he was hurting the woman he loved. "But it was for her own good he thought to himself.

"Sash listen, I'm not tryna hurt you. I'm trying to spare your feelings. I don't want to give you false hopes, make you believe that this shit is gonna work when I know that it's not! This game shit is what I'm made for. This game shit is how I'm keeping a roof over my head, this is my livelihood, it ain't that college shit you going to 3 nights a week and sure enough ain't Jeanine habits that keeps me afloat. It's me. It's me succeeding in this mother fucking game. Look, I'm out.' He said moving to the door, as he couldn't bear to look at her anymore.

"I just don't understand what changed, you told me when you were twelve years old that I was the woman that you wanted to spend the rest of your life with." She said as hot tears trickle down her face.

"Yeah well that was a long time ago. I was a silly kid, I didn't know any better. I'm out." James said and walked out the door. He had just pushed Sasha into Sam's bed and that was opposite of what he wanted.

CHAPTER FOUR

"I can't believe you got me sneaking out to this fucking party." Jasmine said as they sneaked out of the house through the back.

"You always talking about what I got you doing, sis I'm not forcing you. Stay your boring ass home." Taylor said.

"Really Taylor as if I'm let you go somewhere by yourself, knowing you're probably gonna run into Tia."

"I'm not scared of that bitch and whether you go or not. I'm going!" Taylor said.

"You know what you're, right. And I'm tired of getting in trouble because your funky ass can't keep your fucking legs closed. So I'll tell you what, I'm gonna go home this way I don't have to worry about getting cursed out for knowing that your nasty ass snuck out." Jasmine said.

Taylor hissed and turned the other way, then stopped to see if she would change her mind.

Jasmine dialed James' cell phone as she stood on the road. Sometimes she didn't like going home without James. "Hey James, where'd you go?"

she said into the phone.

"I had to take care of something Jas was sup?" James asked still a little upset.

"Are you going home or coming back here?"

"Why Jas was sup?" he asked.

"Oh, sorry. I was just asking because I wanted to go home. I never brought clean clothes here and I left my book bag." She said.

"Ard Jas, go head. I'll be there in a few." James said.

"You promise J? If you're not coming I'll just stay here. You know I don't like being in that house without you." Jasmine said.

"Jas I'll be there!" he huffed into the phone and hung up without saying bye. Somebody pissed him of Jas thought, looking at the phone.

"So you're really not going." Taylor said from behind.

"Nope. See you later bitch." Jasmine said as she walked away.

James just parked his car on a street close to

Ant's but he just sat there trying to clear his head. He decided he needed a different kind of therapy so he called Shantel. He slept with other women to keep his feeling for Sasha at bay.

"Hey Baby." She whined into the phone.

"Yo I'm on my way." He said into the phone.

"Okay, are you hungry..."She began to say but James cut her off. James didn't need the care he already had that from the women in his life. He was going there for one reason and one reason only, sex. James and Shantel had been fucking around for years now, and he had no intentions on it becoming anything more than what it was. Shantel didn't see things that way. In her eyes she was his woman. To him she was a way to pass time, till he was ready for something serious. He showed up to Shantel's only for her to want to talk about where they were going in their relationship. "If Sasha didn't blow my high Shantel definitely did." He thought to himself as he got into his car.

He left Shantel's place and went straight home. He peeked in on Jasmine around 12:30, saw she was sound asleep then dozed off for a few hours before his phone rang waking him up.

"Yo wassup PJ?" James asked.

"Yo! Dawg you was asleep?" PJ asked over the phone.

"Nigga it's 4:30 in the morning what do you think?" James said irritated by his question.

"My bad you can you come get me from Chew and Chelten. I got caught slippin and Shereese flattened my tires and shit." PJ said, a little embarrassed.

"Fuck man! You be in the way nigga. I'm on my way." James said irritated but he just couldn't leave him hanging. PJ and Shereese had one of the craziest relationships James had ever seen. Shereese cheated on PJ as much as PJ cheated on her but they somehow still managed to stay together. Shereese was one of the cutest girls in the neighborhood. She is 10 years younger than him and came from a good family, but PJ had turned her out. She's crazy about PJ and makes a living going through his phone and tracking his every move.

He pulled up at PJ on Chew & Chelten. They drove to the 24hr tire shop off Wayne Ave. "I'm sick and tired of this bitch!" PJ barked, while James just smiled. He had never given his opinion on their situation because he also had a lot on his plate.

"Naw for real J. You wouldn't believe how this bitch acted man!" PJ said still worked up. "The bitch must have put that google tracking shit on my phone again, because I'm sitting in the house with Candice and she is blowing my phone up. I ignore her the first five times; then I'm thinking maybe it's something with the kids. So I go in the bathroom and answer the phone and she is sounding off into the phone. What bitch am I with and all of that? So I try to play it cool, you know like, 'Why would I answer the phone if I was with a bitch?'"

"She ain't fall for that shit huh?" James asked half listening and thinking about Sash and how upset she must be with him.

"Dawg! Hell no she started asking me all kinds of wired questions like, who lives on Logan street, I'm so fucking highed up it still aint hit me that she was outside. So I'm like I don't know. Next thing I know my car alarm is going off. Dawg the bitch was out there beating my car with a bat and slashing my tires."

"Damn!" James mumbles.

"That ain't it dawg! Then she barges in Candice house when I open the door and starts fucking her up. I gotta find a place dawg I'm done with this bitch." PJ said.

James laughed hysterically at PJ, "Dawg you don't think she has the right to act like that, after she just caught you in another bitch's house?"

"That's not the point J, if she didn't go looking we wouldn't have these problems."

Still laughing James asked, so the problem isn't that you're cheating, it's that she goes looking, right?"

"Whatever man you always take her side." PJ said.

"Nah man I'm not taking no sides, you know I don't get into that." James said looking, to see if the mechanic was almost done replacing his tires. It took almost an hour and half to get PJ and his car moving. James decided to go back over to Shantel's, Sasha was too heavy on his mind.

CHAPTER FIVE

"No Dwight please, stop" Jasmine cried out! She tried to fight him off of her but he was way too heavy. She always tried to fight him off. Dwight was her mother's boyfriend who had decided to stay in the house whether their mom was home or not. He was jobless and made no contribution to the bills in the house but they let him stayed because he made their mother happy. For almost a year, Dwight had been touching Jasmine in the wrong places. As bad as she wanted to, she was too scared of tell James. Not because she was afraid of Dwight but because of what he might do and also what Dwight might do.

"Why me? Where's James, where's mama, where is anyone?" Jasmine thought as he tried to force himself on her. This time was different from other times. Her face was wet, she couldn't fight him off if she tried. Maybe if she thought of something else and pretended it was happening that would help. It didn't. "James!!!!" she cried out or at least she thought she did. "Where are you? You promised to be here, you promised to protect me?" She said to an imaginary James. It was over as quick as it started, but it still hurt as bad.

"Remember this is our little secret, because if James found out he would kill us both and end up in jail and I know you don't want that." Dwight said wiping himself with her nightgown and walking out of the room. She laid there paralyzed and couldn't move. She was soaked in tears, sweat and blood. She heard Dwight turn on the shower and she could hear him singing, Marvin Gaye's. 'Let's get it on.' She tried to pull herself off the bed, but couldn't as she was hurting badly. She had always dreamt that her first time was going to be romantic and memorable. Well this was going to be memorable for sure. She thought to herself. Trying again to stand, she's able to even though her legs were numb from the ordeal. Wiping her face, she gave herself a pep talk. "Toughen up. This is your life deal with it." She said to herself. She thought of shooting Dwight herself but she remembered college. James had always taught her to never let people see her sweat. She looked at the clock. "Shit its 8 O'clock Ima be late for school." tipping into the hallway, she quickly washed away the blood and tears. Fixed her hair, applied a little eyeliner and tried to put the morning out of her mind and headed out to school.

"Have a good day Jas." Dwight said as she closed the door.

As she walked down the hallway in school, it felt like people knew what happened to her. It seemed like everyone was staring at her. "Could they tell, did I look different?" she thought to herself.

"Hey Bitch, where were you? I called you a thousand times" Taylor said from behind.

"Only if you knew" she thought. She really wasn't in the mood for her ratchetness this morning and she hated it when she called me 'bitch', Dwight called her that, and momma called her that!

"Hey Taylor." she mumbled, trying to fake a smile.

"What the hell is you problem?" Growled Taylor.

"Nothing." She mumbled again.

"Then why do you look so.... So spaced out." Taylor asked curiously.

"I'm just tired that's all." Jasmine replied.

"Well where you were this morning?" Taylor asked irritated at the fact that Jasmine was giving her a one-liner.

"I overslept damn!" Jasmine yelled.

"Bitch I'm just asking, but since you wanted to be super bitchy last night and this morning maybe I should throw away your homework that I got for you from Mr. Pierces class!" Taylor replied with a grin.

Jasmine couldn't help but laugh, Taylor was a pain in the ass, but she always had her back. "I'm sorry T." Jasmine replied with a smirk.

"You're welcome, you know you my girl." Jasmine was glad she escaped Mr. Pierce's class, she hated asking him for anything because he looked at her the same way Dwight looked at her.

"So how was the party?" she asked Taylor to change the subject. She needed a form of distraction. All of a sudden Taylor became excited

"Bitch! That shit was so lit! Brian nut ass didn't come. I saw that bitch Tia but she knew better, she stayed in the corner with her dusty ass girlfriends rolling their eyes all night and shit. I had Caprice meet me since you bailed out on me and she aint fucking with

Caprice! But girl I had a fucking ball. So how did you sleep last night with ya boring ass?" Taylor teased.

"Fuck you Taylor." Jasmine said laughing. They both walked to the door of Jasmine's English class. Are you staying all day?" Jasmine, asked Taylor knowing she only did half days in school.

"No, I'll see you at lunch then I'm going to Brian's." Taylor said with confidence.

"Ard." Jasmine said, shaking her head as she went into her class.

"Shantel what the fuck? I told you to wake me up at 7!" James said angrily as he jumped off the bed.

"I know baby, but you looked so peaceful I didn't want to wake you, plus you never get any rest." she said in the sexiest voice possible.

"Baby but you know I hate disappointing Jas, she does everything right and all she ask is that I'm at the house every morning by 7:15 to make sure she is up and get breakfast." James said as he began to gently kiss Shantel on her neck. Most mornings started this way because, James found Shantel so sexy he could barely keep his hands off of her and Shantel knew. "Babe listen I gotta go." James said, pulling away before things got out of hand. "I will holla at you later." he said hurriedly trying to avoid the argument, he knew was coming.

"Why babe? Jas is already at school, don't go." she said.

"Don't do that" James said.

"Do what? You don't have to go if Jas is already at school, unless you're running to lay up under Sasha." She said with an attitude. She knew James was also in love with Sasha and she hated it so she tried every trick to always keep him with her.

"Don't start your shit Shantel, that's why I hate coming cause you always on some bullshit." James said as he threw on his sneakers.

"What motherfucker? If you don't like coming here then nigga don't come!" she yelled and threw a pillow at him. "I ain't sweating you, as a matter fact nigga, you're right. You do have to go, roll out!!!" She yelled.

James walked out of the door quietly, knowing that by later tonight she'd be over it. Jas was way more important than Shantel so he had no time to explain to her. On his way in he stopped by the gas station, and grabbed her an instant oatmeal cup she liked.

"Jas!!!" He yelled as he got in.

"Naw James she been gone, I woke her up." Dwight said. James really couldn't stand Dwight because he introduce their mom to drugs. They had been together for about ten years, at one point they were both shooting heroin. James had put them both in rehab a few years back but it didn't last long.

"Oh ok good." James mumbled, "Was she late?" He asked, trying to be nice since he was nice to Jas, he thought. Always buying her sneakers and clothes, not that she needed them because James made sure she had all she needed.

"Uh yeah but maybe just a few minutes I think." Dwight replied.

"Why are all these lights on? Jas room is empty, why are the lights on?" James yelled.

"Uh, Uh I will turn it off." Dwight said hurriedly as he scurried up from the couch to Jas room to turn the lights off.

Dwight always get super nervous when James get pissed, because they never saw eye to eye and James ran the house. Although James tried not to mess with him, because his mom really loved him and no matter how low she got he's stayed and looked out for her.

"Ay Dwight when's the last time you saw mama." James asked.

"Just this morning I saw her coming out of the basement." he said

"FUCK!" James screamed cutting him off mid-sentence. "She found my fucking stash." He said under his breath. He tried to move it around the house throughout the week. James quickly ran down the steps as fast as he could. "Shit! She had definitely found my stash." James said to himself as he checked his stash. He never left much money down there. The little he left was for Jasmine in case of an emergency. He wasn't too worried because he knew that she wouldn't take all of his money, she might have taken a lot but no matter how bad she's doing she would never leave them high and dry.

After counting what was left, he calculated that she took about a stack from the money. He had to find somewhere else to hide it so that Jas could always get to if it she needed it. He chuckled as he realizing that Jeanine must have watched him last week as he went to get some money out for Jas and Taylor to go to the mall. He laughed at the idea of his mom watching him. He thought of hiding the remaining stash in Jasmine's room, she never goes in there because she and Jasmine always fought about space and territory. He decided to hide it in one of Jasmine's old shoe box. He decided to go check on Sasha. He felt bad about leaving her especially after the way he talked to her the previous night.

CHAPTER SIX

Taylor and Jasmine had been friends since they were kids and she knew when Jasmine was keeping something from her and it got her worried. Taylor may not seem level-headed but she loved Jasmine so much. "Could she still be upset with me from last night" she thought to herself as they met for lunch.

"So where did you end up last night?" Jasmine asked breaking her train of thought.

"You would know where I was, if you would have listened to your voicemail! I spent the night with Jared." She said biting her lower lip.

"Yo Come on T, like what the fuck? I know you not fucking with Jared." Jas said looking at her with scrutiny.

"I absolutely am! Why what is it to you?" Taylor asked acting all defensive.

"What is it to me? When Shanice finds out its war and you know it, you keep putting yourself in these nut ass situations! Like I just don't get it! Them bitches' aint got shit going for themselves, all they do is fight over these nut ass niggas." Jas lectured.

"Jas please your forever talking like your better than somebody, what the fuck? What do I actually have?" Taylor said angrily. She hated it when Jasmine lectured her about making it out of the hood and doing better than the next person. Always talking about college and all, she hated it so much.

"Taylor what do you mean what do you have? You are beautiful and you're smart. That's your problem as long as you believe that you're average you'll be just that, Average!" Jasmine replied. She didn't like the fact that Taylor didn't see beyond sleeping with men for pleasure or money.

"You think that now Jas! Mrs. Honor roll, Mrs. fucking college scholarship I don't have any of that shit!" She screamed. "So yes, I FUCKED Jared and I fucked him good! And to be honest Jas I don't give a fuck about Jared Shanice or any other bitch that he fucking and furthermore..."

Her words were cut off by a sharp blow to the head. She never saw it coming! Stumbling she could hear voices. She heard Jasmine's voice and a few other voices that she didn't recognize. Trying to regain her composure, she swung wildly and grabbed a lock of somebody's hair, pulling them to the ground. She looked for Jasmine in the crowd and spot her beating the shit out of some chic, just as the girl reached for a blade. She screamed for Jas to watch out. Just as Mr. Pierce ran in their direction, taking Shanice down to the ground then security showed up, pulling Jasmine off the girl.

Taylor was surprised as she watched Jasmine beat up the poor girl, she had never really been in a fight and even when there was one she would avoid it. Taylor ran over to calm her down as she reached to grab her, Jasmine screams and hits her in the face, at that point Taylor knew that something was going on with Jasmine. Jasmine continued wailing, it took about three staff members to calm her. After finally getting Jas to calm down, Mr. Pierce had them seated in his office, while they tried to piece together who the girls were and what had happened in the hallway.

Jasmine sat with a blank look like she was in another world.

"Jas, are you ok?" Taylor asked. She looked at Mr. Pierce, then back at her.

Just as Jasmine started to move closer to her, Shanice walked by screaming in handcuffs and Jas went after again. Before anyone could react Jas grabbed a pair of scissors off of Mr. Pierce's desk and stabbed Shanice in the back. She managed to knock the scissors away from Jas, and the guards took her to the office, just as James and Sasha walked through the school gate and went down to the office to check on the girls.

They were together over at Sasha's place when they received a call that there had been a fight involving Taylor and Jasmine and a girl had been rushed to the hospital.

"What happened, what the fuck happened?" James yelled as he entered the office.

"I'm sorry James, I'm so sorry!" Jas said amidst her sobs.

"James, look Shanice and some girls faked liked students who had lost their ID to get in school to fight us. They snuck me! But we fucked them up though, but James Shanice had a blade she tried to cut Jas and…" Taylor rambled on scared that Jas was going to lose it all because of her.

"Taylor shut your mouth! It was all in self-defense, and Jas is a minor she was threatened. Do you understand?" Sasha said cutting Taylor off. Taylor shook her head yes, to let her know that she fully understood.

"Taylor, Jas let's go!" James said.

"Unfortunately Mr. Williams Jas and Taylor have to stay here until the police arrives." Mr. Pierce said. "Police! Police!

Man listen my sister is not talking to no damn police I don't give a fuck what you're talking about." James said furiously.

"James, James listen please. It's best for Jas if she cooperates. I know you're scared for her but James, Jas is 14 and Shanice is 20. She was trespassing and Taylor said she had a blade." Sasha said.

"Yes she did! I swear she did! Mr. Pierce saw it too." Taylor chipped in. "They will probably just take a statement we can follow her to the station and she should be released." Sasha assured James.

"Mr. Pierce can vouch for Jas, can't you?" Taylor asked, with an eyebrow lifted. Unknowingly to Jasmine, Taylor had been sleeping with Mr. Pierce for a while now. He gave her whatever she wanted money, clothes, booze and even good grades. He knew he had no choice but to say yes because Taylor could put him in greater trouble.

"Of course Jas is a model student and I believe she was frightened for her life." Mr. Pierce said. The security guard who had Shanice handcuffed began to speak to disagree but Taylor also gave him the same look she had given Mr. Pierce and he shut his mouth because he also knew better. See this is one skill that college could never teach her, she thought.

Jasmine just sat there blanked out from the rest of the world as she stared at the handcuffs. "How did I get here?" she asked herself. "This has truly been the day from hell, first Dwight, and now this bullshit with Taylor." She thought. She looked up at James and for the first time in her life she could see that he was frightened. She hated the fact that she was the reason for his fear. Her lip began to quiver as she thought about the day.

"Hey! Toughen Up!" James said with a weak smile.

CHAPTER SEVEN

After hours of questioning she was released but Unfortunately it wasn't over. Shanice was pressing charges and she had to appear back in court. The car ride home was horrendous but Jasmine was thankful that they were staying at Sasha's and Taylor's that night. At least she wouldn't have to see Dwight. She thought. She went straight to Taylor's room when they arrived, she needed a moment to regroup. The day was just too much for her.

"What was up with you today?" Taylor asked.

So much for that Jas thought. She wasn't in the mood to answer any questions but she felt Taylor asked her a very stupid question.

"What do you mean what was up with me today?" She asked angrily. "The question is what's up with you. Have you lost your fucking mind? My fucking life could be ruined all because you can't keep your fucking legs closed." Jasmine yelled hoping she'd back off.

"Who the fuck do you think you're talking to?" she yelled back. "I didn't ask for your help. You could have taken your fucking punk ass to class like you usually do when some shit pops off. Don't blame your actions on me, blame that shit on the fact that you woke up on the wrong side of the fucking bed!"

"Bitch who you callin a punk. Ima fuck around and go to jail because I tried to stop you from getting your ass beat. I could have let them bitches jump you! Oh but forgive me for being a real friend! Bitch! But I know for the next time. Why don't you do us all a favor, put your fucking knees together bitch and keep them there. If your dumb ass could follow those simple instructions you won't end up in no bullshit." Jas said very angry.

"Bitch fuck you, you will be turning tricks just as often as me the moment you get the heart to let somebody run they dick up..." she blacked out and jumped on Taylor flailing before she could finish her sentence. "Bitch get the fuck off me! Are you crazy?" Taylor screamed trying to get Jasmine off her. But Jasmine was sick of her and couldn't stop herself from swinging. She was so angry, she hated her and hated her own life.

"What the fuck is going on?" James said as he

bursts into the room. "First y'all fight at school now y'all fighting each other?" James asked, totally confused.

"Jas are you ok?" Sasha asked gently, "What's going on with you today?" Jasmine didn't respond but began to cry. James says nothing he just looks.

"Jas you were saying some strange things while you were swinging and fighting on Taylor do you remember?" Sasha asked.

"What? Fuck I had gotten Taylor in trouble. I never meant for Sasha to hear those things." She though in her head and continued to cry. "Jas listen you can talk to us, its ok we are here for you." Sasha said. But she just continued to cry. "Taylor is none of those things that I said." Jasmine said.

"Jas what are you talking about, Taylor is none of what things?" Sasha asked.

"None of the things that you said you heard." She repeated.

"Jas while you were sitting on top of Taylor you were screaming 'No, No stop please don't hurt me.' Do you remember that?" Sasha asked. What were you talking about? Is there any reason why you would say those things?" Sasha asked. She shook her head right and left. "No." Jasmine answered knowing it was all because of Dwight. She looked up at James and saw the worry all over his face.

"Let me talk to Jas for a minute alone please." James said with his eyes on Jasmine. He sat on the bed next to Jasmine as Sasha and Taylor left the room.

"What's going on Jas, you know I have your back." He said as the door closed. Jasmine nodded her head. "Have I ever lied to you?" he asked. She shook her head no. "Then be honest with me. Is anyone doing something to hurt you?" he asked. She stayed quiet. "Jas please I need to know it's my job to protect you and if someone is hurting you I will put an end to it. So again is anyone hurting you?" James said.

At that moment she decided not to tell James what Dwight had done, because by putting an end to it James did not mean going to the police! He would kill Dwight himself and if James was arrested she could never live with herself. She hated to admit it but

Dwight was right.

"No James I'm just afraid I will lose my chance at a scholarship if this goes on my record. That's why I was saying those things but it was gibberish because I was so angry." She said as confident as possible. James could easily spot a lie so she tried to be convincing.

"Are you sure?" James asked suspiciously, as she shook her head yes

"Ok but you do know I'm here and we can talk about anything, you know that right Jas?" he asked still worried.

"Yes." she said and they hugged

"I love you Jas."

"I love you to J."

Jasmine and Taylor were grounded for a week. They served a two day suspension, although she knew Taylor had something to do with it but she didn't tell her. There were no charges filed against her but Shanice was still in jail for force entry into the school premises. As the days went by Jasmine also worried about telling her boyfriend about Dwight.

CHAPTER EIGHT

Things around James were getting too weird for him. He see that Jasmine was changing, while Taylor was a lost cause and Sasha was losing her mind. He hadn't seen his mother Jeanine in almost 2 weeks. He thought he always had things figure out, but the week felt like slipping which put more pressure on him to get his family out of the neighborhood. James was losing money in the streets and Broady was planning to go to war. "I gotta get shit together" he thought to himself. His phone buzzed and it was Broady. "Yo Broady wassup?" "Wassup we still meeting up?" He said into the phone. "For sure, I'm headed your way now. I'll see you in 10." James replied. "Ard Bet." he responded before ending the call.

"At this point it's do or die. The streets were drying up and we need money." Broady said. This had been the topic between James and Broady for the past few weeks. He did his best to buy time but it was now or never.

"It's time to take over the city, but Broady listen there has to be a plan in place.

We can't be out here winging it, cause somebody gon get knocked off." James said trying to calm him down.

Broady was extremely smart, but he was also dangerous. He believed that any and everything that was done had to be done with the use of excessive force.

"Come on J, This money taking shit is easy. Everything doesn't require a fucking blue print." Broady said.

"All we gotta do is, catch them niggas off guard. Go at them quick and strong."

"Nah they too heavy dawg." James tried to explain.

"This nine will bring those niggas right to their knees. They bleed just like we bleed. If we swarm them niggas and take them down at once, we'll already be in place before them niggas can recruit or recuperate." Broady said with a wide grin.

"Nigga I get it! The point I'm trying to make is that, if and I mean if we do this shit! We have to be mentally and physically prepared for war. This shit aint gon be easy." James said raising his voice.

He knew that Broady was right the only way for them to get back on was to take down Jamal's crew. But James was strategic, they needed a plan.

"Nigga you don't think I know that?" Broady fired back. "Listen the heat is on either way. We are fucked up out here. I got kids to feed. These are major players. I been checking these niggas out J, they are moving major fucking weight. I mean bigtime. They already crossed the line by bringing that shit across the bridge. Them niggas got work on every block from 33rd street to now 21st St. We need parts." Broady explained.

"Ard let's get with PJ and Roc and pull some shit together." James said.

"Bet!" Broady said with a smile.

"Broady!" James Barked

"Yo J!"

Don't do shit without my approval." James ordered.

"I gotchu." He said smiling. The whole idea excited him. This was the kind of shit he lived for.

James just couldn't shake the feeling that, this was a bad move. But he had already committed to it, and truth be told it was the only solution he could see. As much as he knew, he needed to get back to Sasha's to check on Jas, he didn't feel like dealing with any emotional stress so he headed to Shantel's. Shantel was all over him when he got there. James was so thankful that there was no drama. Finally a peaceful night.

His phone woke him up, he moved away from Chantel to pick the call.

"Hey Sash was sup?"

"Hey!" Sash answered.

"Are you home?" she asked.

"Nah wassup though?" he answered and rolled his eyes because he knew what was coming next.

"Nigga you really need to get it together. I was just calling because Taylor is gone already and I've been calling Jas but she's not answering."

"When did she go home anyway? Last time I talked to her she said she was staying there." James replied.

"Yeah well, she left here shortly after you yesterday. She said she was going home to pick few of her things so she could study, so I just asked her to sleep over there since it was late."

"Oh ard." He was aware of her exam that morning. He hoped she didn't over sleep.

"I told Taylor to go there first but that's like talking to myself. And now her ass ain't answering either." Sasha said.

"Oh yeah, they better not be on no bull shit." James said.

"Well if you were there like you're supposed to be then you'd know what time she got up. But you too busy chasing ass. Call me and let me know that she made it on time when you get there." Sash replied and ended the call before he could respond.

He jumped up and into his clothes, told Shantel he was out and closed the door before she could start tripping. "Not Today" He thought to himself as he hopped into his car. Surprisingly there was no traffic, doing 60 down Broad St, he turned on Flamerz 2 by Meek Mill and headed home. The way these girls kept him running he began to doubt if he'd ever have kids of his own. He pulled up to the house, left the blinkers on, hoping that Jas had already left and he could run over and check on Sasha to try to calm her down.

He paused as he ran up the steps, he almost couldn't will his feet to move to the next step. He knew what he heard, however he couldn't understand it. Moans? Or Muffled Cries? "But from who?" he thought. Their mother Jeanine had been long gone and then it hit him, 'Jasmine!' As fast as his legs could move he skipped steps to get upstairs. "I will fucking kill her!" he thought, "How foolish could Jas be bringing a nigga in here knowing that I'm liable to pop up at any time?" He hit the top step and reached to his waist band for his gun.

"Dwight?" he whispered as he heard Dwight's voice. If Dwight had decided to bring another woman into his mother's house, honestly that was between those two, he thought. He tucked his gun away, and moved closer to Jas's room. James heart dropped to the floor seeing Dwight holding his fourteen year old sister down, with his hand over her mouth. Jasmine saw James and closed her eyes, before she could reopen the them, James pulled the trigger. The first shot hit him in the head. He watched as he fell away from Jas. She scrambled away from him and pulled up a sheet to cover herself. James moved closer, pulled the trigger again, this time hitting him in the back, again and again. He shot him until the gun clicked. He could hear Jas scream, but all he saw was Red. The vision of Dwight hurting his sister played over and over again in his head. He snapped out of it and could see the fear in Jas's face. He wasn't sure if it was because of what Dwight had done to her or what he had done to him. They had to get out of there he thought. Hurriedly he told Jas to grab as much stuff as she could and go straight to Sasha's.

"Listen to me! Don't say a word to anyone about this do you understand me?"

James said as he held her. She shook her head solemnly, in the moment for the first time he could see pain in her eyes. God was has she been through. After Jas left James hopped in the car. He drove with no destination trying to calm himself and think of the next step. Eventually he ended up at Sasha's. When he finally walked in, he found all three of them huddled up in some kind of embrace on the chair. Jas couldn't and wouldn't even look up at him.

"Give me a minute with her." he said.

"No James please let them stay, they know everything." Jas whispered.

James just sat there staring at his most prized possession. All broken. He didn't know what to say or what to do. He wanted to hug her! But he just couldn't. He was too numb.

"How long. How long has he been doing this Jas?" James asked trying to avoid crying because his heart was broken. Jasmine started to cry, he wiped a tear before it could fall.

"That nasty motherfucker had been touching her for more than two years, James." Sasha said.

James lost his breathe! He felt like going back to the house to shoot him some more.

"Two fucking years?" he said. Afraid to say anything for fear of hurting Jas further but he couldn't understand why she didn't say anything before now.

"This was the second time he's actually gone further than touching her and ..." James raised his hand cutting Sasha off before she could finish. He couldn't take any details at the moment.

"I'm sorry." she whispered.

"Come on Taylor." she said standing up. Jas looked up at her pleading with her eyes for her to stay.

"You guys need some alone time to try and sort things out." Sasha said before leaving the room.

James moved over to the chair and put his arm around her and pulled her into an embrace. He didn't know what else to do because he knew nothing he did would change what Dwight did to her.

"I'm sorry Jas, I'm so sorry! I didn't know." He said as a tear dropped from his eyes. He just couldn't control his tears. His tears triggered hers and she cried so hard that her body shook. "You could have told me Jas, You should have told me." He said pulling himself together.

"How did this happen? Does Mama know?" He asked.

She shook her head no. It all begin to make sense to James.

"Is this why you never wanted to be home without

me?" he asked. She looked at him and said, "Yes." The more he remembered things the worse he felt.

"This shit happened right under my nose and I was too caught up in these bitches and these streets to even see it." He thought to himself.

"God Jas I'm so sorry. I wish I could go back over there an empty another clip into that niggas body." James said, holding her and rubbing her shoulder.

Sasha walked into the room, to inform him that the cops were at their house. She had received a call from her friend Kima.

"James what are you gonna do?" Sasha asked.

"They will come here next." He said. He got on his feet, thought for a second and said.

"Jas go upstairs and get washed up. Put on some PJ's. Sash listen to me. I gotta go get out of these clothes and get the car cleaned out. I'll be back tonight, then me and Jas is gonna have to go lay low for a minute."

"What? What do you mean?" Sash asked

"I can't just hang around Sash and wait for them to figure out what happened. And I'm not leaving her alone, not while she's like this. I have to protect her. I was supposed to protect her."

"James she wouldn't be by herself, I'm here." Sasha said insulted.

"I'm sorry Sash that's not what I meant." James said. "I gotta go." he said. Before he walked out he looked back at Jasmine and she shook her head to let him know that she understood. As soon as he got out of the door he called Ant.

"Yo meet me at the spot." He didn't even know how he planned to explain this to him but he was the only person he could trust with this.

Ant just sat there, dumbfounded after James filled him in on what happened. He just couldn't believe his ears.

"That nigga got exactly what he deserved, and I wish I could have been a part of it. I can't stand a pervert." Ant said angrily.

Ant helped him get the car cleaned, and volunteered

to drive he and Jas to a motel outside of the city. They pulled back up to Sasha's and asked Ant to wait in the car.

"Hey are you ready?" he asked avoiding eye contact. Shaking her head she grabbed her duffle bag, and got up to hug Sasha and Taylor. Sasha started crying which he expected. He moved to her and put his arms around her.

"Listen we are gonna be ard! We will be back soon. We just have to lay low until I can figure out if I'm a suspect. Keep your phone on ard?" James said trying to reassure Sasha.

"Ok, I love you James."

"I love you too Sash, and Taylor don't think cause I'm absent you can be out here showing off." He said only half way joking. She ran and gave him a hug. The four of them have been a family for years. A dysfunctional family, but still a family.

They hopped in the back of Ant's car and lay down in the seats.

"Where should I take yall?" Ant asked.

"Just drive Ant I don't even know. James said trying to clear his head. Just get on the highways there are more cars."

"Ard bet."

After what seemed like an eternity even though it was an hour he looked up and saw signs that said welcome to Maryland. Perfect he thought, it was quiet out here. James told Ant to stop them at the next motel and head back to the city before somebody noticed that he was gone.

"Ard J hit me on my hip if you need me." Ant said referring to his pager, while getting in the car.

"No doubt! One!" he said. They checked in and Jas went straight to bed. All he could do was watch Jas sleep. He tried to think back to the times when things were good. He thought about everything again and wondered where the hell Jeanine was.

CHAPTER NINE

"Move it Bonnie, move it you're not getting any of my shit." Jeanine screamed getting up to move away from Bonnie, her crack friend.

"No!" she said shaking frantically like she had just seen a ghost.

"No is right you didn't put in on this, shit I borrowed a lil money from James stash. I'm gonna pay him back when I got my check next week." Jeanine said. She knew he was probably mad at her so she stayed away from the house till she got her check.

"Nooo! Jeanine listen, there is a whole lot of cops at your house I mean a whole lot. Not like just normal cops either. They are wearing all kinds of fancy shit." she said. She had gone by Jeanine's house earlier and saw cops and the ambulance.

Jeanine was forty-three years old and despite her drug abuse she was still stunning, in a rough sort of way. Her beauty was once the talk of the town but now she was just a shadow of herself. She had James when she was nineteen and Jasmine when she was twenty-eight for two different men, she refused to tell her kids.

She dropped everything in her hands and just began running. She was running and praying at the same time. "Lord please let my babies be okay." She prayed. She looked back and could see Bonnie scrounging to pick up all of the drugs and money she had dropped.

Walking up to her house and seeing cops and ambulance vehicles everywhere was a real awakening for her. All she could think of was James, "What if he was dead?" she thought to herself as she pushed her way through the crowd to get into the house, with tears in her eyes. She had already lost one child and she couldn't take losing another. Just as she got to the steps they came out with someone in a body bag. She froze with as she imagined her baby with gunshots to the head.

"Ma'am do you live here?" An officer asked. She just responded with a nod.

"We need you to please come identify the body." He said pointing to the ambulance. It was then she noticed Pee Wee, Dwight's friend sitting in the back of a police.

"Do you know him ma'am, the detective asked?"

"Yea." She managed to whisper.

"We found him in the house covered in blood.

Pee Wee had always been jealous of Dwight, since way back in the day. Jeanine had dated Pee Wee long ago, and he never got over the fact that she ended up with Dwight. The only reason they even became friends is because they got high together. But there was always some problem or another between the two of them.

But even with all of that Jeanine couldn't figure out what issues he could have with James. Had he tried to rob him for drugs? She asked herself so many questions as she climbed up into the back of the ambulance to identify the body. She held her breath as the officer grabbed the zipper. She never thought she would see her son this way, and it was no one's fault but her own, she thought to herself. James would never be hustling out in these dangerous streets if she wasn't on drugs. Everything bad that James has ever done has always been in the best interest of his family.

"God please!" she cried in her heart. For the first time in probably ten years she began to pray. "Dear Lord I know I haven't been the best child and I haven't lived the best life but if you could take me instead, please do. James doesn't deserve this." She prayed in her heart as tears rolled down her cheeks.

"Ma'am, Ma'am!" the medic said, bringing her back to planet earth. She looked down at the body in the bag and she had mixed feelings.

She felt relief and pain at the same time. She was relieved it wasn't James, and she thank God. But she felt pain because it was Dwight, her love. Her heart ached at losing Dwight and her tears continued to roll down her cheeks. He wasn't the best man in the world but she didn't think he'd ever done anything to warrant anyone murdering him, and certainly not his own friend. It had to be the drugs. She thought to herself.

She fell to the ground, and just cried as grief overcame her. Not just for Dwight's death but for all the wrong things that had ever happened in her life over the years. She cried for James although he was alright, she cried for the life Jas had at her expense. She cried for Dwight, She cried for her mother. "Momma" she thought to herself. She hadn't thought of her in about twenty years.

The Paramedics and officers ran to her and tried to pull her up.

"Are you ok Ma'am?" one them asked. She shook her head no, because she wasn't.

"Do you need medical attention?" he asked.

"Yes." She shook her head with her hands over her face ashamed of herself and what she has become. "It's time to hold up my end of the bargain to God. I have to kick this shit and pull things together for my children, they need me, and they deserve to have me." She said to herself.

Jeanine was asked if she wanted help with her drug addiction and she said yes, she just wanted this phase of her life to be over. She thought of calling to warn James and Jas not to go to the house. But they always seemed to find out things faster than her so she decided to let them be. She wanted to see them when she was okay, especially after what she had done to them. She was sure someone had told them what was happening, she would wait to see them when she was better.

Although initially admitted at Temple hospital she was eventually transferred to Mercy Hospital in West Philly where she was admitted into their inpatient drug program.

"Ms. Crenshaw if you are a hundred percent ready to commit yourself to this program and to change we do have a bed available." An attendant said as she stepped into facility.

"Yes, yes I am committed, can I stay right now? Please don't let me walk out that door because I won't come back. I don't think I'm strong enough to come back." She said as a tear trickled down.

"Yes ma'am, Ms. Crenshaw you can be admitted right now. Is there anyone that you'd like to call?" She dropped her head,

"No there isn't." She said in almost a whisper.

She knew James and Jas had had enough of her, and had run off to Sasha's, they had finally gotten fed up with her. She felt not just bad, but ashamed because she had taken Jasmine's lunch money and stolen James money from the basement. She stole from her own children, she shed a few tears thinking of them and how they must be feeling now.

"It's ok most participants enter the program alone, after they have successfully completed treatment their families are more willing to give them a second chance. Although you may feel that you have been selfish already in your addiction, I need you to be selfish just a little bit longer. This program focuses solely on you." Lisa the intake specialist said.

"Ok, fine by me." She muttered.

"We start from the inside out. We leave no stones unturned. When you leave our program it will be with a fresh start." She said with the biggest smile while standing to give her a hug and escort her to her room.

"Before we get settle in is there a place where I can be alone to pray." Jeanine asked. As Lisa led her down the hall.

"Sure I'll show you where the chapel is, you'll have 24 hour access to it. You never have to ask permission to use it." She said.

"Okay thanks." she replied.

"I'll wait for you right out here." she said as she sat in a waiting area adjacent to the doors of the chapel. Jeanine took a deep breath and walked in, although the other day had been her first time praying in years there was something comforting about, so she vowed to do it more often.

 She knew God didn't switch James body with Dwight's in that moment but she was certain that it was by the power of his grace that James was still alive. She knelt down in the middle of the aisle just to think, and her life began to flash before her eyes. Losing her father, and her best friend. Her children were everything to her, and yet she had let them down, but she was done running. She was done letting all of the pain and grief knock her down, not anymore she thought to herself.

"Amen." She said as she ended the prayer. She felt renewed

She knew that this time she was done for good, she was ready for a new day and a new her. She was ready to heal, ready to be a mother and ready to be better.

CHAPTER TEN

Jasmine waited until she could hear James breathing heavy and was sure that he was asleep before she moved. She couldn't bear to look at him and see the pain on his face. Pain that she had caused. It had been a week since they fled Philadelphia and it was beginning to bore her. She understood they had to leave but she missed a lot of things. She moved as slowly and quietly as she could to use the bathroom. She got in there and just for a while trying to clear her thoughts, trying to erase the image of Dwight raping her and James shooting him dead. She could still smell his blood.

She tried to think back to happier times, when things were right with them before Dwight came around, back when momma smiled, and was stable and around. Even though she was much younger she could see it, her mother's beauty. She missed her so much. Her voice was different and happier, she could still remember when she read bedtime stories to her and taught her to pray. God how did things change so drastically, she asked. She stood to leave the bathroom but then felt herself begin to kneel. "God, grant me the serenity to accept the things I cannot change, the courage to change the things I can, and the wisdom to know the difference. Amen." She prayed. That was their mom's favorite prayer. "Jesus!" she yelled and jumped as James knocked at the door.

"Jas are you alright in there?" James said through the door.

"Yes I'm fine I'm on my way out." She said. She turned the water on to wash her hands and splash a little cold water on her face, before heading out.

She opened the door to the TV on and room service.

"When did you do all of this?" she asked, surprised at the activity that went on without hearing. She must have been caught up in her thoughts, she thought to herself.

"While you were in the bathroom praying and stuff." James replied.

"How did you know I was praying you were listening?"

"Well not exactly. I was coming to ask if you were hungry and I heard you talking so I listened. I miss mom too." James said.

Jasmine smiled and took a seat in front of the food.

After about ten minutes of watching her push her food around on her plate for a while.

"I guess you're not hungry." James said.

"No not really." She replied.

"Look I know..."

"Please James not now, I can't I'm sorry." She said cutting him off.

"I understand, just know that when you're ready to talk I'm here." James said touching her hand.

"I know. I do have a question."

"Yeah what's that?"

"Where is my cell phone?"

"I have it. You can't be calling people Jas your phone may be tapped or traced even. I will get us new phones tomorrow. But who are you trying to call?" James asked.

"Who else? Taylor and Sasha, they will be worried sick by now." Jasmine said. Telling only part of the truth. There was one more person, Cam. She had sent him a text before leaving town that they were going to an aunt's place for a while.

"Yeah I got word back to Sasha through Ant. But listen we gotta lay low for a while. I'm mad as shit that I even got you hiding out with me but I can't take the chance of you slipping up talking to them or the cops." James said.

James watched her for a while then said.

"If anything ever happens just promise me that you will l tell them, I forced you to come with me."

"I would never James, never!" she snapped back. "Let's talk about something else, please." She said.

James sighed and smiled. He knew it was wise to change the subject if not they would start arguing.

"So tell me, are you sure you only wanted to call Taylor or is it that 324 number that been calling your phone all night." James asked.

"Huh?" Jas said, acting like she didn't know what he was he was talking about.

"Ain't no huh Jas. I keep telling you I ain't dumb, and you aint no good at lying. So who is he?" James said.

"Nobody James." "Come on I'm your brother you can tell me." James teased.

"It's nobody James." Jasmine said laughing.

"Okay keep ya little boyfriend a secret, Ima find out who he is and Ima bust that lil nigga right in his head." He said jokingly and Jas laughing out loud.

James loved that she was laughing again, and he would give anything to help her heal.

"Ard let's get some sleep. First thing in the morning I will get us some burnouts so you can talk to your little..."

"Taylor!" she giggled and screamed.

"Yeah ok." He said raising his hands in defeat.

"You take the bed Ima take the chair."

"NO!" she screamed frightened "Uh you can sleep in the bed with me just get down the other end." She said.

CHAPTER ELEVEN

It's been two days and they had only left the room once. Jas made sure James was sleeping before she snuck to find her phone. She checked his pockets then finally found it at the bottom of James duffle bag. She snuck into the bathroom to call Taylor and instantly Sasha answers the phone. "Damn!" she thought. She just froze with the phone in her hands.

"Jas, Jas I know it's you. "Jas please say something, let me talk to James."

"Uh you can't. He is sleeping and he doesn't know that I've been using the phone if he finds out he will kill me."

"Too late." James said from behind her and she almost jumped out of her skin.

"Fuck! You scared me James."

Wide eyed James asked "Who are you talking to Jas?"

"Sasha and Taylor I just wanted to tell them that we were ok."

"Give me the damn phone. Dammit Jas!" She gave him the phone then he put it to his ears.

"Hello? Oh God, James are y'all alright. I was so scared that something had happened to yall."

"No we are straight hasn't, Ant been over there to relay my message."

"Yeah, he stopped by but James but that was three days ago. I mean really what the fuck were you thinking leaving me in the dark like this."

"Sasha this is why I didn't call I can't go through this shit right now I got too much on my mind."

"I'm sorry James, I was just so worried. I just can't bear the thought of losing you losing yall."

"Ard Sasha I gotta go this phone could be tapped."

"Alright I love you guys be safe and promise that you'll call me soon James, please."

"I promise."

"Ok bye."

"Oh wait Sash"

"Yea?" She asked.

"Have you seen my mom?"

"Oddly enough I haven't and I was just telling Taylor

the same thing."

"Has everything been cleaned up and shit down at the house?"

"Yea it looks like it."

"Ok listen this is what I need you to do. I need you to go down there and knock on the door."

"Ok"

"Make sure no one is looking and lift up the floorboard closest to the door, you should be able to raise it with your foot. Don't take it all the way but you should see a key if you see the key good leave it there and leave. But if the key isn't there that means momma has been there and I need you to go in the house and make sure that she isn't in there ......" James said but his voice trailed off as he thought of her overdosing because of Dwight.

"Ok but what do I tell her if she is there?" Sasha asked bring in back.

"Tell her I'm sorry and that we are okay and tell her we will see her soon."

"Ok."

"I call you tomorrow around this time but from a different number, so be sure to answer your phone." "Ok I will. I love you James." She said in a way that warmed James' heart.

"I Love you to Sasha." He said and quickly hung up.

CHAPTER TWELVE

"Taylor!" Sasha screamed from the living room.

"Yeah?" Taylor answered from her room.

"Come ride with me somewhere."

"Ok here I come, can we get food please?" Taylor asked as she rushed downstairs.

"Taylor please can you think about anything else Jesus." Sasha said, shaking her head. Sasha actually planned to stop to get something to eat because she didn't feel like cooking. She hadn't felt like doing much of cooking since James left.

They pulled up in front of Jeanine's before going to get food. Sasha got out of the car nervously scared of the worst.

"Stay here Taylor, I will be right back." Sasha said as she closed the door.

She kicked up the floor board just as James had asked, but the key was missing and this scared her more. She checked her purse for her spare, and unlocked the door. A lump formed in her throat as she was petrified to go in.

"Lord knows we can't take anymore tragedy." She whispered to herself and found the courage to go in.

"Hello, Jeanine! Are you in here Jeanine?" She whispered standing close to the door.

"Jeanine?"

"I think it's empty." Taylor whispered scaring her.

"Didn't I tell you to stay in the car?"

"Yeah but I got scared."

"This is so weird, like do you see how clean it is in here?" Sasha said walking around the apartment.

"The last time I'd seen it clean like this, shit we were kids." Taylor said also amazed at the transformation. "Ok Taylor let's go, this is creepy. I'll let James know once he calls tomorrow." Sasha said ushering Taylor out and locking the door.

"Well when he does call tomorrow can you please ask him if he'd let my best friend call me." Taylor said with good girl smile.

"Yeah whatever."

"Jasmine please I will be right back I got to pick something up." James said.

"Why can't I come with you to town?" Jasmine asked.

"No it's too dangerous. Just stay I'll be back." James said and walked out the door. As soon as he got out the door he called Ant.

"Yo meet me at the spot and bring like 20K with you." James said.

"On my way, you good?" Ant asked.

"Nah man, not at all. I holla at you when you get there."

"Ard Bet." Ant said and hung up.

They were running out of cash, from paying for the motel and food. He couldn't wait til this shit blew over. He could see that the boredom was driving Jas crazy, but they had no choice. He also thought of getting them burner phones, so he could call Sasha time to time, to keep her mind at rest.

Jasmine waited for about fifteen minutes

after James left before she started rummaging through their things in search of her phone. She prayed and hoped to God that he had left it behind somewhere. She checked his duffle bag but it wasn't there, she checked everywhere but couldn't find it. She thought of the places he liked to keep things so she thought of checking his shoes.

"Whew!" she sighed as she found the phone.

She quickly sent Cam a message to meet her at a mall about thirty minutes away and told him it was emergency. She needed to see him and be back in the house before James was back.

She held onto the phone like it was life itself as she waited for his reply. "Buzz!" her phone buzzed.

She checked the message and it read, "On my way."

CHAPTER THIRTEEN

Jas missed Cam so much; she couldn't wait to see him. She needed some real love and manly attention. Not that she didn't appreciate her brother's love but she just needed to see another face. The moment James told her he was meeting up with some people she just had to seize the opportunity. Although she was careful not to give him their location because if anything went wrong James would kill her. She walked around the mall just to pass time as she was about ten minutes early. She was aware it would take Cam about forty minutes to get there but she just couldn't sit still in the motel.

Her phone buzzed and it was Cam. He sent a text saying he was in the parking garage. She rushed down to her baby and the moment she saw him standing by his car, she ran towards him jumped on him.

"I missed you too Baby." Cam said as she hugged him.

"I missed you so much." Jasmine said kissing him as a tear dropped, but she quickly wiped it.

"I know baby, but I can't breathe." Cam said as she held his neck very tight. She quickly let him and they both laugh.

"Come on let's get into the car. Cam said as he opened the door for her.

Camelot was twenty-two years old. He grew up on the street. He was Jamal's best friend and right hand man. They had been friends since they were kids. Camelot's parents died when he was a lot younger, so he was raised by his grandmother just as Jamal was. He always felt that if they were alive he would probably have been a lot different but he couldn't change it and wasn't even complaining. He loved what he did and it wasn't just for the money. He just loved the idea of being in control. He and Jamal got in this game under some true old heads and been in it for a long time now.

Cam had caramel colored skin and hazel eyes. He had beautiful wavy hair which he mostly wore in cornrows.

"So what you been up to, Damn? I fucking miss you."

"Nothing much, spending time with my family, bored." Jas lied.

"And your aunt?"

"She's cool." Jas replied.

"Well you must be having a good fucking time, shit I ain't heard from you, let me find out you got a little side nigga out here." Cam said

He knew Jasmine was a lot younger than he was and some people may see this as wrong but he didn't. Despite their age difference he'd fallen in love with her, and had been really going through in her absence. Although he had plenty other girls to keep him entertained, it was something about Jas that he just couldn't shake, and what made it so crazy is that he hadn't touched her sexually at all yet.

She was a good girl unlike her friend Taylor who had slept with almost everyone in his crew. He also didn't want to put pressure on her as he was also scared of taking her innocence, because he was scared of hurting her in the end. Jasmine had always thought of college, although it all sounded stupid to him He like that she had goals and ambition. That was rear where they grew up.

They went to get something to eat and talked for a long time before Jasmine leaned in to kiss him.

She sat on the back of the car while he stood between her legs. He kissed her back and immediately his body became warm as he felt her soft pink lips. How could a girl have so much power over him, he thought. He pulled closer to her and kissed her passionately while she ran her hands through his hair and down his back.

"Don't stop, please." Jas said as he parted his lips from hers.

"Baby, I want you more than you could ever imagine" Cam chuckled "but did you forget where we are."

"No I didn't, we are in a dark parking lot, where nobody can see us." Jas moaned, leaning in to kiss him again

Kissing her back, Cam scooped Jas up and got into the car.

He took off her T-shirt and his eyes widened as he saw her small firm breasts. He took off her bra and his mouth watered more once he caught sight of her bare breast. He took one in his mouth and she moaned loudly. Caressing her with the other hand, they both begin to lose control. The car was a little bit cramped but he didn't care he just wanted her. He took off his pants, took her hands and put them on his now erect penis so she could caress him.

"See what you do to me." He whispered into her ears.

She had no experience but her touch was enough. He pulled her skirts up and pulled down her panties, so he could touch her. He stopped as he was about to slid in and asked,

"Are you sure?" Remembering that in previous conversations she had told him that she was a virgin. "Yes." She whispered back.

There was no use keeping what was broken, she thought to herself. He slid into her carefully in order not to hurt her and rode her gently till they both climaxed.

Jasmine walked to the motel all smiles with a bag of chips in hands. She needed to wipe out her experience with Dwight and it worked. She'd always remember this day with Cam as her first time. This time it was more pleasurable although it hurt at first but later it was all fireworks. Jasmine was also happy that he didn't really seem to notice that she wasn't a virgin anymore. She had been worried he would notice and that she was no longer a virgin. She just couldn't wait to tell Taylor that she did it.

She unlocked the door to their room and turned on the lights.

"Shit!" she screamed as she saw James sitting on the chair.

"What the fuck James you scared me."

"I scared you? How the fuck do you think I feel! Where have you been?" James said raising his voice.

"I just went to the mall to clear my head, that's all James."

"That's all, what the fuck did I tell you? Why can't you just listen, for once?"

"Cause I ain't a fucking pet that you can ask to sit, James. Gosh!" she said her heart pounding. She moved to sit on the bed.

James looked her down and said, "Give me the

phone."

"Huh!" "Give me the goddamn phone now. Let me see who the fuck you been talking to." James said. Jasmine swallowed hard and handed the phone to him. She had hoped she would be back before him. James scrolled through the call log and text messages but found nothing. He checked again and stared Jasmine down.

"I don't know why you can't trust me, I wasn't talking to nobody. I just took the phone in case you came back and was worried." Sasha said with a little confidence. She thanked God she had remembered to delete the calls and text messages they exchanged.

"Look I know you tired and shit but I need you to do as I say, especially now that we hiding."

"I know James I just went to the mall." She said.

James just stared at her because he couldn't really tell if she was lying or not, but there was something a little off. She seemed to be in a good mood, maybe she that time to herself.

"Anyway, I kinda got good news."

"What?"

"That nutcase, Pee wee was caught in the house and was arrested for the murder."

"Yo you serious. Does this mean we could go home?"

"Nah not yet, we still can't find ma and the child services would probably be snooping around and shit. Look just give me some time till all of this is blown over I'll make it up to you. Ard?" James said and she nodded yes with a dampened spirit.

CHAPTER FOURTEEN

After leaving James ran down to Broady at his mom's crib to update him on what was going on with James and to deliver his instructions. So far Ant was the only one that knew that James was hiding out. If word got out that he was out of town, it would leave them vulnerable. James had instructed Ant to fill Broady in.

"Wassup my nigga." Broadly said as he opened the door.

"Aint shit." Ant responded,

"Aye listen I just wanted to let you know that we are holding down the fort, a little longer. "

"What you mean?" Broady asked.

"Well J got into some shit and had to put a nigga down so for right now he's laying low and we on top."
"Say no more bro." Broady responded, shaking Ant's hand.

"With that being said, Ima make my way back to spot to get some work to put out here on these streets. We running low like a motherfucker. I hope this shit blows over soon so J can get back and put this plan into motion." Ant said. Broady joined him as they walked down the street.

"Exactly! I mean I know J is out of town but we got to make a move. We can't just sit around and chill while these niggas just take over our streets man." Broady said as he brought out a joint to smoke.

"You right bro; we just gotta cut J some slack you know." Ant replied.

As they stood there talking they didn't notice two masked guys heading towards them. Suddenly everything went dark, as they were hit over the head and knocked unconscious. When Ant woke opened his eyes he could taste blood on his lip and Broady was lying unconscious across from him on the floor. He realized that his hands and feet were tied, "Fuck!" he mumbled.

They had been so caught up in talking they never saw it coming. Broady started to groan and Ant was relieved that he wasn't dead.

"Yo Broady, get up man." He said kicking at him, but he was far away. He felt a sharp pain in his ribs as he tried to untie himself, he could feel that his ribs were fractured if not broken.

Broady finally came to and they were able to untie each other.

"Shit!" Broady screamed, as he tried to get up. Ant reached for his phone to call Roc.

"Yo Roc, we got hit man."

"What? Where you at? Who you with?" Roc asked in a panic voice.

"Me and Broady were headed to the spot to re-up and some niggas ran down on us. It had to be those 21 street niggas."

"Damn, are yall good? How much did they get?"

"Yeah we good, a little beat up but we good. Man they got everything!"

"Yeah! Everything?" Roc asked.

"Man they got every fucking thing Fuck!" Ant said.

"Shit!" "Yeah I know. It's lights out for them niggas. I'mma holla at you in a minute I'm getting ready to hit J up and see how he wants to handle this.

"Ard one."

Ant thought of calling James but didn't even want to disturb with this drama, and wasn't. He needed to be there for Jas right now. After locking everything up, Ant and Broady made it back to the car.

"Yo man drop me off at Tish crib. I don't even feel right going straight to my mommas. Those niggas might still be on my tail." Broady said.

"No doubt, but listen. J got a lot of shit going on right now. I don't really want to put this drama on his head too, along with everything else.

"Right I can dig that.

So what do you suggest we do?" Broady asked

"You already know. Its lights out for them niggas.

Right!

Listen lay low for the rest of tonight. Hit roc and them and let them know to watch their bodies out here because these niggas on our heads and I'll get with you tomorrow. Ant said

"Ard Bet"

"If you need me I'll be at Irene's" Ant said as he

dropped Broady off. Although he tried to reassure Broady that them niggas probably took off but he didn't feel comfortable going to his baby mom's house either. He couldn't expose his children like that, so he drove to Irene's place.

"Damn babe what happened to you?" She asked as she opened the door and saw Ant's face. She had opened the door all smiles but it all diminished as she saw his face. "Nothing just go into a little scuffle."

"With who?" She asked.

"It's cool don't worry about it."

"Are you sure? Who was it your nut as baby momma?" she pestered.

"Yo will you chill out!" Ant yelled irritated by her questions.

"She always fucking you up and you always coming running to Rene to be the good doctor right?" she continued.

"Never mind yo I'm out." Ant said grabbing his jacket and moving to the door.

"No, no baby I'm sorry. You know Irene don't mind taking care of your ass." She pulled him towards the chair and pushed him into. "Let Irene show you she's sorry." She said dropping to her knees and undoing his buckle. His pants and jackets dropped at the same time. Exactly what he had come for.

CHAPTER FIFTEEN

It had been two months now and she was already tired of doing nothing, she missed school, Stupid Taylor, Sasha and of course Cam. She had woken up to 10 missed calls from Cam, and she needed to call him back. She checked around the room and saw that James was out so she quickly dialed him back and of course he didn't answer. Oh well she thought. Going into the mini fridge to eat some of James leftover chicken from last night. Before she could even get it in her mouth, she felt sick. Making it to the toilet just before she vomited all over the floor. Splashing her face with cold water she thought she must still be queasy from the greasy cheese steak the night before.

James had been giving her a little freedom, allowing her to go to the mall and movies alone. Thinking that she needed alone time to clear her thoughts.

Of course she spent each and every one of those days in the parking lot with Cam. Cam couldn't understand why he couldn't come to her Aunt's house or why they had to stay out there so long.

Jas worried that he would get tired of her seeing as though had a reputation of having girls at his beck and call. It was hard to talk to him being holed up in one room with James. She dialed his number again,

"Hey babe" she said into the phone. It felt so good to talk to him.

"Wassup Babe." he said. She could hear the excitement in his voice. "Damn I miss you."

"I know babe I'm sorry." She answered

"You still outta town at your aunt's?" He asked.

"Yeah but we should be home soon." She lied.

"Soon like when soon like tonight cause I need to see you baby."

"No not tonight." She said closing eyes because she knew exactly what it was that he needed and she needed it to.

"Where you at?" She asked.

"I'm at the mall tryna cop something to wear to Capone's party tomorrow night."

"Oh you tryna get fly for the neighborhood bitches huh?" she teased.

"Don't start your shit Jas, you already know I aint worried about none of these little dusty bitches." Cam said laughing.

"Yeah ok, where is the party at anyway?" she asked, a little jealous.

"Vanity Grand." he answered

"I should have known, wherever there is naked bitches, there are thirsty niggas."

"So you just gonna call me a thirsty nigga?"

"Well not you, you said you ain't worried about them hoes.

She could hear James coming down the hall on his phone. "Ard babe go ahead and do what you doing. Ima hit you back later and stay away from them hoes."

"Ard babe talk to you later." He said and she hung up.

"Was sup?" James said coming in with breakfast, "I see you're finally up. You been sleeping pretty hard." She just smiled at him, and tried to hide the phone.

"I got your favorite he said, turkey bacon cream chipped beef pancakes and scrambled eggs. I mean it ain't mamas but it's something right." James said with excitement.

"Uh huh." She said shaking her head yeah and

reaching for the platter as she was starving.

"Aye who were you just on the phone with?"

"Nobody." She answered a little too quickly

James knew she was lying.

"Jas I heard you talking to somebody. Listen you don't have to lie to me and I'm not expecting you to not talk to anyone. I was just asking to make conversation.

"It was Taylor J."

"Oh ard. Listen we are not on the run, the cops aren't looking for us, yet anyway. I'm just trying to make sure that no social workers or no shit don't show up tryna place you in a home. So as soon as we find momma we can go back home." James explained.

"Well can I go back into the city tonight, a girl from our school is having a party and Taylor is going." she said.

"Jas are you sure you're up for that I mean..."

"James I'm fine."

"Come on Jas you can't just be fine. We still hadn't talked about the other day. You know you can talk to me"

"James." she interrupted,

"I don't ever want to talk about that. It's over, and that's all that matters." She said and kept stuffing her face.

"Okay, look Jas I really don't feel comfortable driving back into the city so soon and I don't want you there either."

"I figured you would say that James. I mean James couldn't you just let Sasha come get me, then I could spend the night that way you don't have to drive back to the city tonight you can just pick me up tomorrow. If I'm still around it won't look like we are in hiding." She said and smiled as he pulled out his phone to call Sasha.

"Hey Sash." he said into the phone and Jasmine could hear her screaming his name as if he'd been gone forever.

"Ard I'll tell her to get ready." he said while hanging up the phone. She started to jump around the room in excitement, not only because she was getting out of the cooped up room but because she knew she was headed straight to Cam's.

"Chill out, listen Jas, seriously. Sash ain't far she was out shopping with Kima at the outlets. She should be here within the hour so get your stuff together. Keep your phone on so I can check on you. I'm gonna have Sasha drop y'all off and pick y'all up at the party." James instructed.

"What no James that's embarrassing come one." She protested.

"What do you mean embarrassing yall are 14 years old. It's too crazy right now you're not walking through the streets this late at night, so make sure you tell Sasha."

"Ard." She said just to shut him up.

She really didn't give a fuck about what James was talking about, she texted Cam "I'll be there tonight, be ready" she hit the power button on her phone to black out the screen and packed her bag.

Just as she finished showering and putting her clothes on, Sasha called James to say she was outside. She ran out of the car so fast with James behind her. She was hoping she would pull up and pull right off, but Sasha ran to James and hugged him like she hadn't seen him in years. Rubbing his face and asking him if he was ok. Jasmine just laughed at her, "Thirsty ass" She thought.

"Sash will you chill, I'm good!" James said.

"Are you sure? Come home everything's been quiet."

"Not yet Sash, have you seen or heard from Jeanine?" James asked.

"No J not at all, do you want me to go check on her?" "No I don't want you going down there again."

"Ok well just let me know." she said before going in to hug him again, before walking towards the car. She waved at James and could tell that he was worried about Jeanine.

Jasmine was also worried about her mother as she had never gone missing for this long before. She tried to take her mind off it and concentrate instead on how to get to Cam's place.

As soon as they pulled up in front of the house Taylor came running out of the door.

"Jassssss, Oh my god! I missed you so much!" she screamed. They jumped up and down and danced outside for what seemed like forever,

"OMG I missed you too, we have soooo much to talk about." Jasmine replied dramatically.

"Are you back for good? Please say your back for good."

"No I wish, I'm here until Sunday."

"Why, when are you coming back, I mean yall are coming back right?"

"Yeah we are, but I don't know when, cause James keeps saying soon. He's afraid the Department of Public Welfare will come and take me since I'm under the age of 18. And if they do I'll Run."

"Right." she said as they finally took a seat on the steps, "But how is everything else."

"Good." Jas replied.

"I mean with you and James after all of that Dwight shit." Taylor asked, concerned for her friend.

"I'm Good Taylor, the motherfucker is dead and I'm glad. James on the other hand I'm not sure. He's weirded it out and weirding me out. He's being overly nice, constantly asking me if I'm okay and shit."

Jasmine said.

"Well I'm sure he's just worried about you." Taylor said.

"Yeah I know but I just want to put all of that shit in the past. The fucking pervert is dead. Let the memory die with him."

"I hear that. But any who Bitch I missed you and you're back in the city so what's the move?" Taylor asked.

"Well tonight, I need you to cover for me, so I can go see Cam."

"Damn I ain't see you in 2 months and you running straight home to get some dick, that nigga done turned you out." She said laughing.

"Any who Bitch I'm proud of you." She said smirking and they both burst into laughter.

"It's cool we'll just tell Sash we are going to hang with friends from school, she's been so caught up in that nigga Saul since James has been gone, she won't care." Taylor said.

"Yeah? She's into him like that?" Jasmine asked.

"Yes chile had the nerve to bring him here to meet me, with his corny square ass nigga." Taylor said laughing. "He showed up in a blazer, a turtleneck, some jeans and boots and I'm like nigga it's July." Taylor said and Jasmine also started to laugh.

"Wow." Jasmine said "I'm a bit surprised, as she was all up on James when she picked me up."

"Really?" Taylor asked as she laughed out loud.

"Yes girl they hugged for like fucking 5 minutes, if Kima wouldn't have interrupted she might have forgot I was out there."

"That is freaking hilarious, I believe you too she's always frauding." Taylor said.

"Did she cook?" Jasmine asked.

"Nah she's been out shopping all day with Kima. It's her birthday weekend. Their old corny asses are talking about turning up." Taylor said as they walked up the stairs. Just as they entered the house her phone buzzed, it was Cam asking if she was in the city yet. She quickly responded telling him to meet her on 22nd street in 30 minutes.

"Are you hungry?" Sasha asked as they stepped.

"Yes I'm starving, but me and Taylor were gonna hang and grab something to eat." She said quickly, remembering that Cam would be on his way soon. Sash loved to cook, and she knew if she let her get in the kitchen she'd be there for hours.

"Okay love." Sasha said and suddenly pulled Jasmine into a hug... "Oh baby I am so sorry! I missed you so much. Are you ok?" Sasha asked.

"Sash! Leave her alone god! You're so annoying." Taylor yelled.

"I'm ok Sash." Jasmine said smiling.

"Are you sure?" she asked, rolling her eyes at Taylor, "I have been so worried about you."

"Yes I'm fine."

Ok good, you know I'm here if you need to talk."

"Okay." she said then signaled to Taylor that it was time to go.

"Let's get out of here Jas." Taylor said rolling her eyes at Sasha.

"Ard now y'all come home at a reasonable time and be careful you know they finally let the little girl out of jail." She screamed as they walked out of the door talking about Shanice.

They laughed on their way down the steps as they remembered the ass whooping they gave her.

"Ain't nobody worrying about Shanice's Lil, bald head ass" Taylor said, causing them to erupt in laughter. "So where are you going?" Jasmine asked.

"To see a friend." she responded with a smirk and a side eye, as they approached the corner. "Ard call before you head home." Jasmine said hoping into Cam's car and chuckling because she was whoever Taylor was going to see she shouldn't be seeing.

"Damn baby! Wassup?" Cam said flashing his award winning smile as she got in the car.

"Hey baby." she crooned, leaning in to kiss him. "I missed you." she whined.

"I missed you too." He said pulling out of the parking spot.

"You good? What the hell was going on that you had

to go out of town for weeks?" He asked.

"I told you my uncle died." she said with a little attitude.

"Ard, I was just asking. Shit family members die everyday but people don't just get ghost for two months."

"Well we were close, and we had to get the money and stuff together to bury him. And we couldn't just leave my aunt like that. Things just took a little longer than we expected."

"I hear you." He said. He felt something wasn't adding up, but he didn't want to offend her. They pulled up to the house and Cam watched her from behind and noticed she had added a little weight.

"Damn you been eatin out there huh baby...you getting hella thick." He yelled out laughing

"Whatever" she answered back rolling her eyes and walking through the door.

"You hungry?" he asked, as new went through the kitchen.

"Yes I'm starving." Jas said.

"Ard I'll be right back."

 Grab this before it fall babe." He said walking back into the room, trying to juggle the sodas and the plates of food. Jas grabbed the plate and hurriedly set it down and ran to the bathroom, to throw up. Cam could hear her throw up and was worried, so he sat the plates and soda down.

Knocking on the door,

 "Yo! You good?" He asked.

 "Yes." she answered, turning the water on, "Do you have any mouthwash?"

 "Yeah look in the medicine cabinet." He answered. She came out of the bathroom wiping her mouth and sat on the edge of the bed.

"You good?" he asked again.

"Yeah I don't know what happened. The smell of that food made me nauseous."

    Cam watched her for a while then asked.

"Is that the first time that ever happened?" Cam asked trying hard not to panic.

"Well it did happen the other day, but I think that was because I went to bed on greasy food."

"Jas are you on birth control?"

"No why?" she asked but she stopped to think then realized instantly what the problem could be. Cam knew it was a strong possibility since they had never used a condom, but he always pulled out.

"When was the last time you had your period?" Cam asked.

"Oh god! Cam! Oh god Cam!" Jasmine started to panic.

"Calm down Jas, when was it?"

"Two months ago." Jasmine said covering her face.

"Shit Jas! And you didn't realize that shit?"

"No I'm never really regular, and I'm new to this shit I thought you be would be fucking cautious." Jas said crying.

"Don't you put this shit on me? Fuck!" he yelled.

He turned and noticed that she was crying, he went over to her to comfort her.

"Listen calm down Jas. I'm sorry it just caught me off

guard that's all. Look at me." He said trying to lift her face out of her hands. She looked up at him looking like a baby herself.

"We are going to be alright. You can't be too far along we've only been kicking it like that for about a month and a half. I'm not suggesting anything but whatever you decide I gotcha back ard. You hear me?" he said. She shook her head yes.

"I guess I gotta find you something else to eat." He said.

"No I'm ok, I'm not hungry anymore." she said and balled up on the bed.

"Are you sure? "He said climbing into the bed to cuddle with her, hiding his smile. It was kind of exciting to think about having a little Cam running around, although Jas was still crying, he didn't think she felt the same way.

"What the fuck have I done?" Jas thought to herself. Why me! Taylor could fuck a hundred guys and never get pregnant. I have sex with one guy! One guy and I'm fucking pregnant. She thought to herself. My life is over. She cried to herself. Just that fast my life went from sugar to shit. She had some decisions to make but she couldn't make them right now. She closed her eyes and drifted to sleep.

"Yo Jas, get this phone. This shit been vibrating for like 20 minutes." Cam said waking her up.

"What time is it?" she asked jumping out of the bed putting her shoes on.

"12:15" he said.

"Where the fuck are you going?" He asked.

"I forgot I was supposed to meet Taylor somewhere." she said answering her phone.

"Hey, I know I know I'm sorry." She said into the phone.

"Cam can you take me to Taylors please?" she said.

"I thought you were saying with me tonight."

"Cam I can't, come on please hurry!"

"Damn ard chill the fuck out, you hype to run out of here to party with your little hoe ass friend."

"Cam this is the last time I'mma tell you not to disrespect my friend, and don't worry I'll get a ride" she said angrily, before walking out and slamming the door behind her.

"Fine!" he said, pissed off too.

CHAPTER SIXTEEN

"Damn bitch, how the fuck you gon ask me to cover for you and then don't answer your phone" Taylor said angrily.

"I'm sorry Taylor I fell asleep." she mumbled still pissed off at Cam and herself for ending up in this situation.

"You good?" she asked

"Yeah I'm good." She replied. She wasn't ready to tell anybody anything yet.

"Shit I don't even know for sure." She thought.

"Did Sasha call you?" she asked

"No why did she call you?"

"Yeah but I told her we were chilling and that you were in the bathroom. She wasn't worried, because I answered. In her eyes you're the goody two shoes. But shit is starting to change." She laughed and hit Jasmine's arm.

"Whatever Bye Girl, I could never catch up to you. But anyway listen, now that you got your Cam fix. We out here tomorrow night or what?" Taylor asked.

"Oh lord, what's tomorrow?"

"Some young bull named Capone is having a party tomorrow night and I know he's gonna bring the city out. So you know I gotta be there. Will you go with me?" Taylor asked

"Where is it and where is he from?"

"It's at Vanity Grand and I think he's from over 21st street." Taylor replied.

"Cam might know him." Jasmine said.

"Okay and I didn't ask you to fuck him, I asked you to go with me to his party, and since you all in love with this nigga Cam, if he does know him I'm sure he'll be there. Tomorrow you can sneak up him and see how that nigga act when you ain't looking." Taylor said.

Jasmine smiled as she thought of the idea of sneaking up on Cam. She was in once she realized that Cam might be there.

Just as they got to the house her phone buzzed, it was a text from Cam. "I'm sorry, I know you're stressed out and I am too, but I'm kind of excited. I want you to make your own decision about the baby but I just want you to know that I'd be a good father. Hope to talk to you before you go to bed."

She smiled, and turned her phone off. Time to make this nigga sweat. She thought.

"Oh my god, Sasha are you kidding me?" she asked walking in to find Sasha throwing up into a bucket. "Are you drunk?" Jas asked her.

"Yup." she answered throwing up and laughing at the same time. Sam came out of the kitchen with a wet wash rag and put it across her head.

"She called me; I could barely understand what she was saying. Whoever she was with left her at the bar like this. So I picked her up. I'm gonna get going I just didn't want to leave her alone." Sam said before heading for the door.

"Ok thanks." Taylor said with a smile as she walked him out. He was kind of fine when he dressed normal. She thought to herself as she checked out his print through his grey sweatpants. Sasha better stop playing.

"I cannot believe she is drunk." Taylor said laughing along with Jas, who went to make her sandwich and got her a soda.

"Here take aspirin, so you won't have a hangover."

Taylor said.

"I don't need no aspirin turn the music on, It's time to party!" Sasha said.

"So wait a minute, where is Kima she just left you?" Taylor asked.

"She went to get laid I told her I was good. I knew Sam's bitch ass would come pick me up." Sasha said and they all bust out laughing at the same time. They watched Sasha stumble over to the radio and turn the music on and they laughed at her. They sang danced and twerked until the wee hours of the morning before they all passed out right there on the sofa.

CHAPTER SEVENTEEN

Jasmine woke up to the smell of bacon, Sasha was truly wonder woman, she thought as she wondered how she could have been that drunk and be up at cooking breakfast at 10 in the morning.

"Is that you Jas?" she called as Jasmine made her way to the bathroom.

"Yes she screamed through the door."

"Please call your brother, he said he's been calling you all night your phone was dead."

"Did you tell him that I was in here with you?" she asked as she washed her hands.

"Yes I did, but I did not tell him that I was drunk. I'm so sorry Jas that was so irresponsible of me." Sasha apologized.

"Sasha please, you are young you need to have some damn fun. As a matter of fact we came home to early because I think Sam was getting ready to tear that ass out the frame last night."

"Taylor!" Sasha screamed

"Would you stop talking like that? And Jas stop laughing it ain't funny."

"Sash why would Kima leave you like that though?" Jas asked.

"No it wasn't like that we met at the clock bar but she had already told me she was leaving at a certain time so I arranged for Sam to pick me up. But He got caught up at work and I had to wait a little while. So I decided to have a smooth bitch while I wait, after we had already been taking shots of Tequila. Not good." she said shaking her head from side to side.

"Thanks to my little sisters though for looking out for me.

"Jas please call James and don't tell him I was drunk please." Taylor said, mocking Sasha as she grabbed a piece of bacon and walked out of the kitchen.

"Ding! Ding! Ding! Her phone chimed as soon as she powered it on. Cam had sent her at least 10 text message that started out very sweet but ended up annoying.

"Hey J?" she said into the phone.

"Jas damn how hard is it to keep your phone on. I told you I would call to check on you." James said over the phone.

"James I left my charger there sorry I was right here with Sasha and Taylor, why you buggin?" She blurted.

"Why am I what?"

"Nothing James, just take it easy I'm ok." She said.

"Ard, listen if you want I can come pick you up tonight instead of tomorrow."

"NO!" she screamed "James you said Sunday."

"Ard ard, listen keep that phone on, I'll see you tomorrow."

"Ok bye love you bro." she said. She looked at Cam's messages again the last one made her furious. "Yeah you're probably not answering because you're laying up with your real baby father, a virgin my ass. You think I don't know what it feel like to pop a cherry.

"Fuck him." She mumbled while turning her phone off. He had no idea how bad it hurt her.

CHAPTER EIGHTEEN

Just as James pulled up to the motel with Jas his phone buzzed, it was Broady.

"Wassup Broady? "What! Yall niggas did what!?" James yelled. The guys had jumped on their rivals and this pissed him off it meant they had to go to war.

"Why yo! That's not what I instructed yall to do". He screamed into the phone.

"Yo man what the fuck is ya problem. Didn't we talk about this shit? I specifically asked you to wait for my command." James barked.

"Listen J, I didn't want to tell you because I didn't want you stressing, but somebody ran down on the spot and took us for everything.

"They did what, are you fucking kidding me" James asked screaming into the phone. "And you really thought it was a good idea not to tell me?" He questioned Ant

"James, I know you have been under a lot of stress, I was trying......Broady's words were cut off by James' yelling

"I don't give a fuck what you were trying to do, when the fuck did this happen" he asked

"A few nights ago" Broady answered

"A few nights ago, so we not making no money and yall niggas don't say shit, yeah yall fucking trippin." James said angrily.

"J listen, we planned to get our shit back plus some! But we didn't even approach them like that. We were on our way to get a water ice from kings, when we rode past those niggas. You know the lil cocky young bul that I told you I can't stand. He gave us the finger; we just laughed that shit off. Then as we passed the block I realized them niggas was sleeping. They never even watched us to make sure we were off the block.

"They think we sweet. So I figured it was as good a time as any to knock them off. I pulled over and left Roc in the car and me and Ant ran down on them niggas.

So what it happened a little premature the opportunity presented itself. J them niggas was shook. It was three of them and two of us and them niggas never even reached. But that little cocky nigga he would not shut up. He started talking all this tough tony shit so Ant popped that nigga in the leg." Broady trying hard to hide his excitement but James was no fool.

"So you know we don't have no choice but to make a move now?" Broady said. James knew this day was coming and he hated the fact that Broady had made it soon.

"Exactly fool! Yall niggas just backed us against a wall with no fucking game plan. That's not how this shit works. Them niggas got a army of niggas out here in these streets Broady. We are fucking 20 deep at most. How the fuck are we gonna watch our backs and still make money if we out here at war with these niggas. I'm not even there! Did you think about that! Not good Broady! Not fucking good!" James said and hung the phone.

He instantly dialed Ant's phone, he should have known better. He hated the fact that they put him on the spot, now he had to come up with plans immediately. "Answer the damn phone" James he mumbled under his breath, just as he heard ant's voicemail. He texted Broady letting him know he'd be back in town tonight.

Jamal let's himself into Cam's place through

the back door. He had the key to his house just has Cam had the key to his.

Jamal was about five feet, eight inches tall. Just like Cam, Jamal had been raised by his grandmother. Jamal and Cam were next door neighbors. Cam's grandmother despised Jamal as she thought he was a bad influence. He never knew is mother from what he'd heard she was a junkie all of her life and had overdosed some years back, His father had committed suicide when he was young. He was known in the streets as Money Makin Mal, as he had one of the biggest crews and they moved heavy weight.

He was excited that he would have the house to himself. His grandmother had been acting strange lately but he didn't care because she had just called to say she would be gone for a week, which meant he'd have the house to himself...

        "Come in nigga, I'm by myself." Cam screamed. Jamal had walked in on Cam twisted up with some girl so many times that he now always knocked.

"Wassup Dawg?" Cam said.

"Ain't shit, who you had over there last night nigga, I was blowing your phone up." Jamal said as he started to walk in.

"Chill dawg, what did you get into last night?" Cam asked avoiding his question.

"Shit I was chillin with Capone and them last night, we tried to get with you we were heading out down Onyx but clearly you were busy nigga."

"Yeah I got a little action." Cam said trying to appease his curiosity.

"Oh yeah who, the shorty from the restaurant yesterday."

"Nigga chill was that shit at Onyx lit Nigga!" Cam asked

"It was popping." Jamal's phone buzzed then he stepped away to answer his phone.

"What? That was Capone just called to tell me that them niggas from 23rd street just ran down on them talking about taking the block."

"What? Are you fucking kidding me?"

"Yo them niggas really think we sweet out here. Dom got hit in the leg, nothing major though." Jamal said and called Kevin to find out what really happened.

"So hold up, cause this shit ain't adding up" Jamal said into the phone.

"You telling me that these niggas rolled up on y'all, shot Dom and pulled off! And ain't none of y'all niggas squeeze."

"Nah it wasn't even like that though. Mal listen we standing out here shooting the shit and we notice the car spin the block. I reached for my shit as soon as I saw them because I told you that nigga Broady always giving me dirty looks. But them niggas kept going. Next thing I know we here this nigga say don't nobody move. So they must have turned the corner and parked up because they were on foot. But they had the press on us. It was six of them and three of us.

We didn't just stand there like no nuts though. But these niggas got some real balls, they rolled up on us talking about we can do this the easy way or the hard way, but either way they were taking these blocks." Kevin said over the phone.

"Ard shut the fuck up! Imma call you back."

Jamal was pissed but he smiled because he knew that shit in the streets was about to get real interesting.

"Cam find out who these motherfuckers are now."

"Ard" Cam said and dialed a number.

"These little broke niggas really think that it ok to run down on my block and ride off?" Jamal said hitting the table hard. Cam hung up the phone with all the information he needed.

"It was them 23rd St. niggas. That ain't the kicker. I just found out the little shorty that I been fucking with, is his little sister. And the nigga been fucking Shantel for years. I know exactly where to find that nigga."

"You got the drop on the nigga?" Jamal asked.

"Hell yeah."

"Okay this is what I need you to do, I need you to go pick up Maurice bring him back to the house, Imma call some bitch to come stay with him later, while we take these niggas down. I got some more digging to do tell to niggas meet me on 12th at midnight and bring everybody." Jamal said as he headed for the door.

"Time to make these niggas pay. Ima hit that nigga where it hurt." Cam thought as he dialed Jas's number.

Broady has been watching the house for quite some time; little did Cam know Chantel hated him and his cockiness. James had always known that she had family that ran with James crew, and had sweet talked her into getting the address to where they kept their stash.

Broady sent the message letting them know that the time was now. Everybody arrived within ten minutes as planned. Unbeknownst to James, Cam and Jamal's son were making it into the house through the back door.

James sent Roc and Ant around the back. The rest of us set in the car and waited for the signal. PJ stood guard a few houses down in case something went fishy. We sat for what seemed like an eternity, before we heard a loud crash. By the time we'd exited the van

PJ had already kicked the front door in.

Cam heard the noise as they tried to pick the lock and sent Maurice hiding in the basement while he hid behind the couch. He fired two shots hitting rock in the arm once. Roc fired back, causing Cam to drop his gun in the scramble for cover.

Ant seized the opportunity grabbing him by the neck, just as they begin to tussle, James entered the living room and without thinking he let off once shot. Hitting Cam right between the eyes. They watched as his body fell limp.

"When and how the fuck did he get in here". He wondered.

"What the Fuck J? I thought you said it was clear"

"I don't know what he was doing in here; Broady's been watching the house all day. He must have come in the back door." James said frantic

"Look get to the basement grab the work and the cash. and let's get the fuck out of here" He screamed Go!" James said as he ransacked the house.

Few minutes later he heard gunshots from the basement.

"Fuck Fuck Fuck!" he heard Ant screaming and he ran to the basement scared that he was hit. He froze when he got to the basement door, he could see a small body in a pool of blood.

"Shit a fucking kid. What the fuck! How did this happen?"

"I don't know James; I didn't know it was a kid. How the fuck was Broady watching the house all day and it forgot to mention that it was full of people." Ant said rubbing his head as he was devastated.

"We gotta get the fuck outta here!" They gathered the merchandise and emptied the safes but as they reached for the door, they heard gunshots from outside. They took cover first then checked outside. It was Broady, shooting someone on the floor.

They rushed out and saw Jamal, he was still breathing, so James put another round to keep him dead. Avoiding the spot. They headed to a motel in AC. James took all of the work and they split the cash evenly.

"Fuuuuuck!" James screamed

"This shit is bad! This is why I fucking said you don't move without a plan." He barked at Broady

They all just sat quietly, knowing that he was right.

"Now look, look at this bullshit! We killed a fucking kid! A fucking kid! Do you hear me"   and James headed back to Allentown to the hotel with Jas.

The whole ride all James thought of was the poor kid, he hoped the ambulance got there fast enough, and that the little boy made it. He was an innocent kid.

 "What had he done? He had to get out of this game for real." He thought to himself.

He walked in to find Jas sleeping. Which was a blessing he wasn't in the mood to entertain her. Roc, Ant and the rest of the guys knew to get rid of their phones, and secure another one. He'd just wait for the text that everybody had made it in safely and then he was calling it a night.

CHAPTER NINETEEN

He dozed off for a few minutes and was awakened by Jas saying that she was hungry. He didn't even realize that it was Nine thirty in the morning. He quickly pulled out his cellphone and worried that he missed something last night but there was text that said everybody was safe. Jas had been screaming for Cracker barrel so he hopped up got showered and took her out to eat.

"J?" Jas said.

"Yea Jas." He answered studying the menu.

"Are we ever going back home?"

"Of course we are Jas, we are just laying low until I know that it's safe. I can't take the chance of going back there and the state tries to take you away from me or something." James replied. "Just a few more weeks and we will be back home ok."

"Okay." Jas replied warmly.

"Why? Is it so bad hanging out with your big brother all day, I thought this was what you wanted." He Joked.

"Well it's fun sometimes, but I'm bored and I miss Sasha and Taylor, don't you?" she asked.

"Yeah I do more than you know." James said.

The waiter came to take their order with a warm smile. She was pretty and James could not stop smiling. She returned shortly with their beverages, in the middle of Jas rambling on about missing their mom, the waiter smiled and touched James intentionally as she passed him the orange juice.

He winked at her and they both smiled at each other and as she turned around he stared at her ass as she walked away. After finishing their breakfast they decided to go to the movies to see Cadillac.

☐

His thoughts drifted to Jeanine and he tried calling her again.

"The number you have dialed has been disconnected" the operator said.

His heart dropped because no matter how bad his mother's habits were she would always pay the telephone bill.

There was just too much going on. He was more worried than ever about Jeanine, and he couldn't get the kid from last night off of his mind. He'd been up all night. Jasmine was Beyoncé's number one fan, and he was trying to do anything that will make her comfortable. Beyoncé' featured as Etta James, had Jas geeking. And that was all that mattered. They finished with the movies and went back to their motel room. Just as he was unlocking the door PJ called so he let Jasmine go in and he stayed out in the hallway to talk to PJ.

"Yo! I went down you crib, to try to find Jeanine and your grandmom was in the house, talking about you come home so she could take you to go see your mom." PJ said over the phone.

"Grandmom? What Grandmom?" James asked. To my knowledge, my grandmother is dead.

"Well she said she's your grandmom and that your mom has checked herself into a hospital to kick her habit."

James smiled, it was bittersweet. Shit was falling apart for him, but Jeanine was finally getting herself together."

"Ard PJ thanks for looking out. I don't know who the fuck this so called grandmother is but I'll find out."
"No doubt." PJ said then hung the phone.

That was the most interesting of all the news, she checking into a rehab herself. She hated it and always came out the next. "So this where momma had been hiding" he thought. He was so proud of her. We were going home! He thought, and then thoughts of last night flooded his mind again.

He knew he was supposed to lay low after last night but he had to see this shit with his own eyes! And he couldn't wait!

He ran into the room to tell Jasmine the news and found her crying on the side of the bed.

"Jas what's wrong? What Happened?" Jas had been trying to reach Cam all morning because she saw his missed calls. She didn't even if she was crying because she was pregnant or because she felt something was wrong with Cam.

"James I have something to tell you but I'm afraid that you will hate me." She said.

"Jas what's wrong?" he asked alarmed! "Tell me what's wrong I would never hate you?"

"You know how you've been saying that I been acting depressed?"

"Yeah you said it was because you missed mom right, well I'm about to fix that right now." James said. "NO James listen, I have been sad because I have been trying to reach Cam but he ain't picking up and I got a really bad feeling." Jas said.

"Cam, who is Cam? James asked his heart skipped as he remembered the guy he shot dead last night. What could his sister want with him?

"Yeah what about that nigga?"

"J, that's who I've been calling he's, is my boyfriend."

"Boyfriend? Jas he is too old for you and he is a nothing ass nigga so what da fuck you crying over that nigga for." James yelled.

"James I'm trying to tell you something, but you won't listen! James it is more than that he's the father of my child." Jas said.

James froze! He stared at her waiting for her to correct what she'd said! But she didn't she just kept crying.

"He's the what, Jas? What child?" James said with his voice trembling.

"I'm pregnant James and I'm scared." Jas said hugging her knees.

"What the fuck did you just say!" James was enraged; he just couldn't believe Jas of all people would do this.

"After all that I have done to protect you. Jas I gave up everything so that you could have everything. You carrying Louis bags and walking in fucking Gucci shoes and you couldn't buy a condom. And now what?! I'm supposed to help you raise some fucking snot nose ass kid! Because you got pregnant by a nothing ass nigga! Do you know what he did for living? Do you?!"

"Yes but..."

"But nothing. You knew he was a nothing ass nigga! And you still decided to get pregnant by him. What did I tell you about a nigga in the game? He's gonna end up where? Dead or in Jail!" James screamed like a mad man, not even giving her the space to explain.

"How old was that nigga anyway?" he asked.

"He's was 22 J but listen please."

"22! Listen?! Did you just tell me to listen I'm not listening to shit! Look at you? What are you gonna do now. Damn Jas I can't believe you're standing here telling me this bull shit!"

James sat down defeated! Shit just kept getting worse for him. Not only had they shot and possibly killed a kid. He'd also murdered his unborn niece or nephew's father.

"James you're a nothing ass nigga! You're a fucking drug dealer! Jas snapped!

So where will that leave you! Huh? Tell me? Where will you end up James? Dead or in jail? Because you're doing the same shit as that nothing ass nigga! Somebody is gonna take your ass out too, then what? What about me James? I don't have no daddy; barely got a mama and you're never around!" She cried

He is all that I have James! And I'm pregnant! I need him!" Jasmine screamed and dropped to the floor. She just laid there balled up in a fetal position. He wanted to comfort her but he couldn't. He was too angry. He struggled long enough trying to take care of her, and now she was pregnant!

"Jasmine listen, I know you're angry. But he's not who you thought he was. No sane 22 year old man would fuck with a 14 year old girl. He didn't care about you Jas, believe me! I know!"

"Yes he did James he was different."

"He wasn't Jas, he ran game on you!" "No he didn't James!!"

"Don't say that Jasmine listen, that night before shit with Dwight; I had come back in the house to jump on your case because I heard that them niggas had been asking about you and Taylor. Ant told me that he'd seen Taylor and Cam at Embassy Suite out at the airport. Ant tried to tell me that you were dealing with him too but I didn't believe him! So tell me Jas how could he care about you if he's sleeping with you and Taylor. "

He knew telling her that would hurt her but she had to know. Because if it ever got back to her that I was the one that put a bullet in that nigga, he needed her to hate him enough that she wouldn't care.

She and Taylor would get past that shit.

 "Oh my god you're lying James you're lying!" "Why you would lie?" "Why would you try to hurt me like that?" Jas asked with tears in her eyes.

His heart was breaking watching her hurt like this!

 "Jas I'm not lying, I swear I'm sorry! I shouldn't have told you that right now, but you need to know! Just calm down ok? We will work this out ok? Shit is turning around for us Jas! Are you listening to me? Jas?" Noooo, I hate you! I hate you! She screamed

"Don't say that Jas please" James begged.

She wouldn't even look at him, but he knew if he told her what's going on with mama it would soften her right up.

"Jas, I got some good news." She quickly looked at him and then looked away. "We're going home." "Home? How James?! I thought you were worried about child services." She asked.

"I sent PJ over to the house to check on mommy cause the phone were disconnected and apparently our fucking grandmother is there. She wants us to come home and here is the kicker mommy checked herself into rehab!"

"Oh my god! James are you serious that is good news. So when are we leaving please say now. I'm tired of being cooped up in this one room." Although she was happy about Jeanine. All she could think is that she was going home. She would be able to see Cam. He must be so angry at her for falling asleep last night to not answer her calls all day.

"Yeah now let's go! Pack this shit up!" He said trying to keep her happy; she'd doubled her belonging since they left.

"Jas let me ask you a question, what are you going to do about this baby?" He asked as they packed. "What I am going to have it. Cam knows about the baby and he's ready to be a father." Jas said with a smile.

His heart broke into a million more pieces. What had he done!

If only she knew he was dead. James just stared at her. He would never have the heart to ask her if she was sure the baby belonged to Cam. He just shook his head; as much as it turned his stomach he couldn't get the thought out of his head that the baby could be either Cam's or Dwight's. Those were words that I wasn't ready to say.

"Let's go." He said.

CHAPTER TWENTY

The ride home was very quiet. James couldn't the fact that his fourteen year old sister was pregnant out of his head.

"How the fuck do all this shit happen." He thought to himself. He didn't know if to be happy he killed that nigga or be sad that he had just made his nephew or niece a bastard. That one hour ride felt like four hours, he never felt so relieved pulling up to the house. It felt like they had been gone for two years instead of months. Jas on the other hand jumped out of the car before it was parked, she wanted to meet her grandmother. "Slow down Jas; let me go check shit out first." James said, he didn't totally trust the whole grandmother situation so he made her wait for him.

He walked into an empty house, but noticed there were some difference in the house. "Damn!" he mumbled, amazed at the change. This was the cleanest he had ever seen the house. "Mom!" He called out. "Shit!" he Jumped as Jas snuck up behind him.

"Why are you so hard headed? Didn't I ask you to stay in the car?" he asked.

"Where are they?" she asked, ignoring his own

question.

"I don't know Jas but they are not here." He said

"Are you gonna wait around?" James asked.

"No!" she responded,

"Can we go see se Sasha and Taylor pleaseeeeee?" she begged.

"Fine, go put your things up first." He said.

As she walked up the stairs, she froze and he knew exactly why. She was still traumatized by Dwight and he hated it so much. He just couldn't imagine telling her about Cam.

Just drop it right there Jas, we'll get it later." He said. She did just that and walked right past him and out of the door. He picked a few things and headed to Sasha's place.

"Ah!" Taylor screamed out of excitement as she saw Jasmine and James at the door. She jumped to hug James then hugged Jasmine tight. Sasha ran to the living room and hugged the both of them too.

"Please tell me that y'all are home for good." Sasha said as she hugged Jasmine again.

"I guess we are back." James said and smiled, knowing that was music to her ears.

"God I have missed you." Sasha said as she hugged him again. She went to pull away and James pulled her back in.

Shit had been so crazy, nothing felt better than having her in his arms. He had given this some thought and he was done with the game. He was ready to be everything that Sasha needed him to be.

Pinning her to the wall he kissed her so passionately she became weak in the knees.

Jasmine and Taylor clapped as if they just watched the greatest show ever. Sasha just smiled and walked into the kitchen to prepare lunch. They sat down and ate; James filled them in on this so called grandmother story.

Taylor needed to get Jas alone to tell her about Cam. She hated that she had to give her bad news as soon as she got home, but somebody had to do it.

"Come on upstairs Jas, let's catch up." Taylor said, As

Jas said. They left the room together. James and Sasha knew they just wanted to gossip privately.

James and Sasha continued to catch up until they heard Jas screaming and sobbing.

They ran upstairs to find Jas sobbing into the bed.

Jas, what's wrong?" James asked already knowing the answer. He knew that word was out on the street, but he never thought that Taylor may have information on Cam already.

Jas didn't answer, she just continued to sob.

"Taylor what is going on?" Sasha asked

"Uh, her friend Cam was murdered last night." Taylor replied.

"Who Sasha" asked

"Her friend" Taylor said trying to downplay their relationship. "Shit!" James said pretending not to know. Dropping down to Jas he rubbed her back.

"I'm sorry Jas" James said apologizing for more than she knew

"Who is Cam?" Sasha asked again.

"He was her boyfriend!" James said before Taylor could answer again.

Taylor looked at James with a surprised expression.

"Yeah I know" he said to Taylor. It's deeper than that he explained.

"Jas just recently found out that she is pregnant" he winced. It was painful to say

"Oh Jas" Sasha said, dropping down beside James. "Baby I'm so sorry. Is it Dwight?"

Jas looked up, as the realization of that possibility set in. She got up and ran from the room and out of the house. This was all just too much.

"Shit Sasha did you have to say that out loud" James said, as Taylor ran past them to follow her.

She felt horrible, she had no idea that Jas and Cam had gotten serious. After all Jas hadn't seen him for two months, right. She had been secretly sleeping with Cam. She had run into him one night, looking for Jamal and shit just got out of hand.

"James I'm sorry, I wasn't even thinking" Together they moved towards the door to go look for her. James called Taylor and she told them that they were at the park on 22nd and Cecil B Moore. They walked to find JAs sobbing into Taylors shoulder seating on a swing. Sasha and James stood back for a while letting them be.

"Jas, are you okay?" James asked as he moved towards her cautiously.

"No, I'm not J. Just leave me alone." She said sobbing.

It broke his heart to see his sister cry over a guy he felt wasn't worth it.

"Look Jas, you know I can't leave you alone, Just come home with me. We will figure this all out "James pleaded

"How J! How! He is dead. He is fucking dead!" She screamed and ran into his arms.

"What am I going to do about this baby? It's fucking fatherless!" she said in tears.

"Whatever you decide, I'm here Jas, and you got me always. I promise." James said.

She cried harder remembering Cam saying those exact words.

"J promise me you're done with the game. My heart can take any more pain." She said.

"Shh! Nothing is going to happen, let's go home Jas." he said as he couldn't make her that promise just yet. There were still a few things he had to handle.

James, Sasha, and Taylor took her home. Sasha made her some chamomile tea, with hopes that she could relax and doze off to sleep. Eventually it worked Taylor kept a close eye on her as she laid next to her. James heart was so heavy and he couldn't take it anymore. This had to be the longest day ever.

"Are you Ok" Sasha Asked?

"Yeah, just worried about her that's all" James answered

"I know me too" Sasha said standing

"Try to get some rest, I'm going to bed" Sasha said heading into her room.

The last thing James need was to be alone. He got up and followed Sasha into her room. She reached for his hand with no objection.

Are you sure you're okay J? You look twisted up man."
Sasha said.

James knew that he could trust Sasha with anything.
He begin talking, telling her all about the robbery and
how they killed, Cam, Jamal and a kid mistakenly.

"We killed a kid, Sash." James said as he sobbed
uncontrollably.

He expected her to judge and scold him but all she did
was hold him in her arms and cried along with him.

"Oh James." She said as she kissed his head and held
him. She had never seen James this vulnerable before
and it broke her heart.

"Thank you, Sash." James said as he looked up
at Sasha with teary eyes.

"For what." Sasha said. "You don't owe anything"

"No I do. I been pushing you away but you have loved
me still. I don't know what I'd do without you." He
said.

He leaned in and kissed Sasha.

"I love you Sash."

"I love you too J." Sasha replied as they began to rip their clothes off.

"You are so beautiful." James said as he kissed her from head to toe.

"J, are you sure you want us to do this." She asked.

"Yes, I'm ready to love you the way I should have, all this time." James replied, and took her.

As bad as things were Sasha smiled all through the night as he made love to her, thinking her dreams were finally coming true.

CHAPTER TWENTY-ONE

James woke up to Sasha sitting across from him smirking. He wondered how long he had been out. The stress over the past few weeks made him sleep hard.

"Wassup?" He mumbled.

"Wassup with you?" She said still smiling.

"Nothing what you doing yo?" He sat up puzzled. "You watching me sleep?" he asked, with a smug look.

"Boy don't flatter yourself, I was in the kitchen cooking and heard you in here talking and thought you were talking to me. When I walked in and heard you saying my name I was even more intrigued to learn what you were talking about so I sat here and listened." Sasha said.

"Yeah ard I don't talk in my sleep." James said.

"Oh yes you do and I'm glad to know that you, because now I know to listen more. Especially since I like what I heard." Sasha teased.

"Get the fuck outta here Sasha, what did you hear?" He asked laughing.

"Don't worry about what you said the important thing is I know." She said walking away as his phone started to ring. It was Broady.

James ran to Taylor's room and woke Jas to give her the news.

"Jas wake up, momma is home." James said excitedly.

"What?" Jas asked with sleepy eyes.

"Get dressed we're going home, momma is there right now." James repeated. Jas jumped up as she heard her mom was home. Jas quickly dressed up and rushed downstairs with Taylor.

"We'll be back soon, ard? Now that momma's home, we gotta go check her out before she steps out again." He said to Sasha and kissed her before they left. They hopped into the car and drove straight home.

As they pulled up in front of the house, they saw their mom just as she was about to go in. "Momma!" Jasmine yelled as she rushed out of the car.

Jeanine turned and saw Jasmine. "My babies." She said as tears trickled down her face. She headed towards Jasmine and hugged her, then hugged James too.

"I've been worried sick about y'all." Jeanine said.

"We've been worried about you too momma." James said as he checked her out.

She looked so clean; James realized just how beautiful she was. He kissed her and hugged her tight

"Come in, there's someone I need you to meet." Jeanine said excitedly as she led the kids in. As the got in James and Jasmine could hear the humming of a woman. They went towards the kitchen and saw an elderly woman. As soon as the woman turned to them, James recognized. It took him a minute to place her. But he quickly remembered her as the woman in all of the pictures with Jamal in the house they robbed the other night. So he quickly pulled his gun on her.

"James what are you doing?" Jeanine screamed getting in between them.

"What's she doing here, ma?" James asked.

"She's your grandmother." Jeanine said

"What? What do you mean?" he asked with a confused look

"She is my mother James. Put the fucking gun down." She yelled.

He shook his head no and stared at the elderly woman who didn't flinch. It was obvious she had seen her fair share of violence.

"You said you mother was dead" James said slowly putting the pieces together in his head. He sank into a chair close by as his head began to spin.

"I'm sorry I lied to you but she has been alive all this while. Not just her but she was also was with your older brother." Jeanine said as she began to cry.

"Brother?" Jasmine and James echoed.

Jeanine begin to cry uncontrollably

Dorothy begin to speak

"Please Listen! Your mother got pregnant at 14 and by the time I found out it was too late for her too getting an abortion. I told her that she could have the baby but that she would have to give the baby up for adoption. She protested but because she was under aged I had to sign everything. I gave her son your oldest brother away to a family that I knew that couldn't have children. I also forbade her from seeing the father of the child."

My eyes widened in disbelief, as I began to understand what she was trying to tell me! I adjusted my finger on the trigger. Jeanine cried harder, this was all her fault.

"I pretty much locked her away; she continued to speak. I took her everywhere that she needed to go and picked her up. After three months he still wouldn't let up. He called every day and every hour on the hour. I then changed the number and kept it from Jeanine. She continued to explain

"After three months of seeing that boy on my steps day in and day out I decided that we were going to move. Two weeks after moved. Spade that was your father's nickname. His mother called me and told me that he had committed suicide. He left a letter addressed to me."

"His last dying wish was that I allow you're mother to come to his funeral, I felt horrible. I didn't expect that to happen. I thought it was just puppy love. I never meant to bring so much pain to anyone. I gave her permission and she asked if she could go alone, and I let her go!"

"That was the last time that I saw your mother before she showed up to my house a few weeks ago. Last I'd heard she had moved in with boy's mother and my pride and reputation would not allow me to go back looking for my 15 year old daughter who was shacking up with the dead father of her child that she gave away.

Jeanine called me a couple of time but like her I was very stubborn. I told her that if she wasn't coming home then I didn't want to talk. Last time she called was right after she had you at 17 and said she needed somewhere to stay. I told her there was no room for her and a child. She told me that she hated me for giving her baby away and that she would never do it again she said she would sleep in a car first. That was the last I heard from her. I always asked about her I knew about her habit and I couldn't deal with it so I stayed away. A few years later the woman who adopted Jamal died in a deadly car accident with her husband. Jamal was only injured. In cleaning out her home they've found my contact information and called me. I agreed to take Jamal in and raise him.

"I killed my fucking brother" James mumbled

"What did you say" Jeanine asked seeing James mouth move but not hearing the words that came from them.

He just shook his head

"So where is our brother" Jas asked with tears sliding down her face. All she could think is that, she wasn't so different from her mother. Pregnant at 14 with a dead baby father.

"Jamal is in critical condition, both he and his son." Jeanine said. They were shot the other night during a home invasion.

James almost fell of the chair as those words came out from his mother's mouth. He wasn't dead. This shit just kept getting worse. He didn't know if he should be relieved and afraid.

"Jamal?" Jas asked in a whisper.

"Yes." Jeanine replied.

Jas look to James, "Cam's friend Jamal"

"Yes James said

"Shit!" James said as he dropped his head in his hands. This was all too much he had to get out of here.

He stood and walked out of the door and got in his car.
He drove off thinking Jas would be ok Momma was
back. And they'd all be better off without him, after all
of the damage he'd done.

-To Be Continued-

www.ingramcontent.com/pod-product-compliance
Lightning Source LLC
Chambersburg PA
CBHW020855090426
42736CB00008B/385

* 9 7 8 1 7 3 2 0 9 2 6 0 0 *